GET A LIFE WITHOUT SACRIFICING YOUR CAREER

GET A LIFE WITHOUT SACRIFICING YOUR CAREER

How to Make More Time for What's Really Important

DIANNA BOOHER

McGraw-Hill

New York   San Francisco   Washington, D.C.   Auckland   Bogotá
Caracas   Lisbon   London   Madrid   Mexico City   Milan
Montreal   New Delhi   San Juan   Singapore
Sydney   Tokyo   Toronto

Library of Congress Cataloging-in-Publication Data

Booher, Dianna
    Get a life without sacrificing your career : how to make more time
for what's really important / Dianna Booher.
        p.   cm.
    Includes index.
    ISBN 0-07-006647-7 (pbk. : alk. paper)
    1. Self-management (Psychology)   2. Time management.   3. Stress
(Psychology)   I. Title.
BF637.T5B66   1996
640'.43—dc20   96-24446
                                                                    CIP

1 2 3 4 5 6 7 8 9 0   DOC/DOC   9 0 1 0 9 8 7 6

ISBN 0-07-006647-7 (PBK)

*The sponsoring editor for this book was Betsy Brown, the editing
supervisor was Sheila H. Gillams, and the production supervisor
was Pamela Pelton. It was set in Fairfield by Victoria Khavkina of
McGraw-Hill's Professional Book Group composition unit.*

Printed and bound by R. R. Donnelley & Sons.

*Published in association with the literary agency of Alive
Communications, 1465 Kelly Johnson Blvd., Suite 320, Colorado
Springs, CO 80920.*

McGraw-Hill books are available at special quantity discounts to
use as premiums and sales promotions, or for use in corporate
training programs. For more information, please write to the
Director of Special Sales, McGraw-Hill, 11 West 19th Street,
New York, NY 10011. Or contact your local bookstore.

For my parents, my children, and my husband:
Alton and Opal Daniels
Lisa and Kevin McGown
Jeffrey and Laura Booher
Vernon Rae

Thanks also to my agent, Greg Johnson; to my editor, Betsy Brown; and to my staff for their capable help in keeping the office running smoothly while I hide away to write.

CONTENTS

INTRODUCTION: GET A LIFE

The mass of men lead lives of quiet desperation.—HENRY DAVID THOREAU, WALDEN

Our life is frittered away by detail . . . Simplify, simplify.—HENRY DAVID THOREAU, WALDEN

Time lost is time when we have not lived a full human life, time unenriched by experience, creative endeavor, enjoyment and suffering.
—DIETRICH BONHOEFFER, Letters and Papers from Prison

On September 18, 1994, I finished my typical work day about nine o'clock and drove home from the office to grab a bite of dinner, do some reading, and wrap a few gifts for an upcoming birthday. To cap off the night, my husband and I, both tired and irritable, fell into an argument. We finally kissed and made up about midnight and fell into bed exhausted. Five minutes later, a stabbing pain hit me in the back of the head, and I began to jerk. Violent jerks. Violent jerks that sent my whole body—arms and legs and head—into spastic whiplash. The jerks continued every two to three minutes until I fell asleep in the wee hours.

The next morning I dismissed the incident. No problem during the day as I continued the normal, hectic routine. But again, the jerking began at night when I lay down and relaxed my body. Within a week, I had begun to jerk randomly several times during the work day. I'd walk across the room and my legs would buckle under me, as if someone had sneaked up behind me and hit me behind the knees. Still I tried to continue my work—

managing a business, giving author interviews by phone, delivering speeches, and leading day-long communication seminars. At the end of the fourth week, the jerking started midmorning on Friday and continued every few minutes throughout the day and night. With a week-long trip of training seminars ahead of me, I decided that maybe I should see a doctor before flying out of town.

When we reported to the hospital emergency room, the doctor sounded puzzled, "I've never seen anything like it." He conferred with the on-call neurologist, and they admitted me to the hospital for observation and testing. As word traveled down the corridor, the nurses came one by one to see this patient who jerked hard enough to shake the hospital bed—even in her sleep. And one by one I questioned them, "Is this common?" And one by one, they shook their heads. But they assured me that Velma, who'd been a nurse for thirty years, would have seen it. They promised to send her in when she came on duty at 11:00 p.m. The next morning I awoke to Velma taking my vital signs: to my dismay, she couldn't recall ever having seen such jerking.

For the first time in fifteen years, I doubted my ability to lead the upcoming seminars. My husband made the trip to Pittsburgh for me to conduct the training programs while I stayed home for further tests.

Four months, three specialists, and many tests later, the diagnosis was severe myclonic jerking—due to fatigue and stress. Prescription: Rest and get rid of the stress. That was the one prescription I'd never learned to take. And that was my impetus to investigate the ideas in this book.

Clocks get wound up too tight. Societies get wound up too tight. People get wound up too tight. Clocks break. Societies fall. People adapt. Or don't.

This book is about adapting. Are you confusing speed with success? The speed of promotions? The speed of completing projects? The speed of communication? The speed of travel? The speed of phone calls? The speed of technological advancement? We sometimes get so caught up in the speed of accomplishment that our success surprises us. And disappoints us.

We get so caught up in the speed with which we're accomplishing things that we forget to ask where we're going. And then we're disappointed to find that we have arrived without happiness.

You can't *make* time. You have to *find and redistribute* it. You can become more efficient in what you do. You can eliminate redundant actions. You can omit things from your life. You can give yourself the illusion of more time by increasing your energy to do what you need to do. You can improve your coping techniques for a fast-paced life. You can decrease stress. You can develop inner calmness.

These principles are the basis for the tips you'll find in this book. These tips form the basis of my answer when someone asks me, "How do you keep your sanity with so many things going on?"

We've all heard or read most of the principles of time management. They're not new. When I speak to audiences on getting balance in your life while becoming more productive, I usually survey them to ask how many have attended a previous seminar or read a book on the subject. The vast majority raise their hands.

Most of us don't need to "tighten" our schedule, we need to "loosen" it. Yes, of course, some time management techniques can make us more productive. We tuck more and more into our schedules at the risk of subtracting more and more of the stuff that gives us life. That equation causes the imbalance. The time pressure comes from within, not from without.

Do we need some direction and relief? Yes. According to a recent article in *Fortune* magazine, the corporate world has converted to a 24-hour work day, open for business. Acording to the writer Jaclyn Fierman, you can shop at any of 317 Walgreen drugstores, 410 Safeway supermarkets, and 291 Wal-Marts all night long. And *Time* devoted a cover story, "The Evolution of Despair," to our creeping emptiness caused by more work, more money, and less social connection.

Who are the people shopping around the clock and driving into their garages without seeing their neighbors? The same faceless people standing in waiting lines at the pharmacy, staring at the computer screens, or riding the subways. More and more employees are receiving "pager pay" to be on call night and day. We're on 24 hours a day.

In times of 24-hour duty, 60-hour workweeks, microwaves, satellites, and cellular phones, we have traded our lives away. As we grow more efficient, more wealthy, more isolated, and more technologically dependent, we are becoming more stressed, lonely, sad, depressed. As psychologist David Meyes notes in *The Pursuit of Happiness*, the number of Americans who reported being "very happy" stands at one-third. *Training and Development* surveyed employees and came to the same conclusion: Eighty-six percent said their stress at work was increasing, and 68 percent reported that they were either burned out or candidates for burnout. Two-thirds of us are too busy, too stressed, and too sad.

If you're feeling all wound up—stressed and unhappy—you can blame it on many causes:

- Uncertainty about your job
- Urgency of your work assignments
- Overwork or long hours
- Insensitive or incompetent boss
- Promotion or recognition and high expectations
- Failure
- Personnel problems
- Politics
- Repressed emotions
- Thwarted dreams
- Competition
- Isolation
- No job satisfaction

- Lack of skills
- Conflict in your family life
- Interfering or dependent family members
- Money—too much or too little
- Change
- Disillusionment
- Conflict in personal values

Notice how many of these causes have to do with work.

Yet, we work for good reasons: earning money, security, enjoyment, duty and service to others, status, social contact, personal growth, personal satisfaction—or just because everybody always has and still does.

But corporations themselves are feeling the pinch of the pace. Robert S. Eliot, M.D. and director of the Institute of Stress Medicine (Denver, Colorado), clinical professor of medicine at the University of Nebraska, and author of *From Stress to Strength*, estimates an annual $250 billion productivity waste caused by stress and the related cost of unnecessary illness and absenteeism.

The symptoms of trouble ahead include problems in getting along with those at work and home, the tendency to withdraw emotionally, depression, physical aches and pains, drug use, declining job performance, inability to make decisions, loss of concentration, overeating or loss of appetite, sleep trouble— either insomnia or wanting to sleep too much, loss of interest in things previously enjoyed, anxiety, irritability, loss of sexual desire, exhaustion, hopelessness and the feeling of no choice, and the vicious cycle of go-go-go.

Burnout and stress and the feeling of general dissatisfaction in your life are the result of imbalance. It is not heart-rending hardship but the affirmation of affluence that produces the overpowering choices threatening to engulf our spirit and humanity. It is not stark simplicity but chaotic complexity that creates stress and sadness.

You can *lose* your balance easily—ineffective or inefficient work, too much work, not enough play, not enough purpose, or no meaningful connection with others. You may want to take the time to respond to the questionnaire provided here to determine your quality-of-life index. The lower your score when you total the numbers, the more you're probably feeling the need to make some changes. My guess is that if you're reading this book, you already have qualms about the fast-paced life you're leading.

To a great extent, our life is a summary of our choices. With this book, I'm not advocating living like a hermit on $10,000 a year. But I am suggesting that life is lived best when we exercise the right to *choose* what we want to do with our time. So what follows here is a collection of reflective thoughts and specific how-tos on choosing to be time efficient while developing inner tranquility.

You can *regain* your balance. We spend years cluttering our minds and our lives, so most of us can't expect to simplify our lives and free our minds overnight. But any long journey—even a psychological one—starts with a single step. Balance, satisfaction, and freedom wait at the end of the effort. You'll feel, well, "looser."

Quality-of-Life Questionnaire

I'm pleased with the amount of time my career/work requires in my life.	Not Pleased								Pleased	
	1	2	3	4	5	6	7	8	9	10

I'm pleased with my job; it meets my expectations for personal satisfaction.	Not Satisfied								Satisfied	
	1	2	3	4	5	6	7	8	9	10

When I leave work every night, I generally feel that I have completed all that I needed to have done for the day.	Didn't Get Enough Done							Satisfied		
	1	2	3	4	5	6	7	8	9	10

I'm pleased with my progress in meeting personal goals in my life.	Not Satisfied								Satisfied	
	1	2	3	4	5	6	7	8	9	10

I generally feel healthy.	Often Ill								Healthy	
	1	2	3	4	5	6	7	8	9	10

I generally feel rested and "ready to go."	Tired/Weary							Rested/Alert		
	1	2	3	4	5	6	7	8	9	10

I'm generally in good physical shape for my age group.	Out of Shape								In Shape	
	1	2	3	4	5	6	7	8	9	10

I'm pleased with the relationship I've developed with my spouse or other significant person in my life.	Not Satisfied								Satisfied	
	1	2	3	4	5	6	7	8	9	10

I'm pleased with the amount of time spent with spouse or primary relationship.	Not Satisfied								Satisfied	
	1	2	3	4	5	6	7	8	9	10

I'm pleased with the relationships I have developed with my children.	Not Satisfied								Satisfied	
	1	2	3	4	5	6	7	8	9	10

I'm pleased with the amount of time I get to spend with my children.	Not Satisfied								Satisfied	
	1	2	3	4	5	6	7	8	9	10

I'm pleased with the relationships I have developed with my parents.	Not Satisfied								Satisfied	
	1	2	3	4	5	6	7	8	9	10

I'm pleased with the amount of time I spend with my parents.	Not Satisfied								Satisfied	
	1	2	3	4	5	6	7	8	9	10

I'm generally pleased with the relationships I have at work.	Not Satisfied								Satisfied	
	1	2	3	4	5	6	7	8	9	10

I'm pleased with the friendships I have developed.	Not Satisfied								Satisfied	
	1	2	3	4	5	6	7	8	9	10

Quality-of-Life Questionnaire (*Continued*)

I'm pleased with the amount of time I have to spend with friends.	Not Satisfied 1 2 3 4 5	Satisfied 6 7 8 9 10
My spiritual life is complete and satisfying.	Not Satisfying 1 2 3 4 5	Satisfying 6 7 8 9 10
I have hobbies and outside interests other than family responsibilities and work.	None 1 2 3 4 5	All That I Need 6 7 8 9 10
I have time for all the hobbies and outside interests that I enjoy.	Not Enough Time 1 2 3 4 5	Enough Time 6 7 8 9 10
My weekends are enjoyable and carefree.	Not Enjoyable 1 2 3 4 5	Enjoyable 6 7 8 9 10
I have time to do a good job in fulfilling my family responsibilities on a daily basis.	No Time for Best 1 2 3 4 5	My Best Effort 6 7 8 9 10
I am comfortable with my financial situation.	Heavily in Debt 1 2 3 4 5	Comfortable 6 7 8 9 10
I feel that I have time to relax and enjoy life.	Overwhelmed 1 2 3 4 5	Relaxed/Comfortable 6 7 8 9 10
I feel satisfied with the amount of control I have over my life.	Trapped/Out of Control 1 2 3 4 5	In Control 6 7 8 9 10
I'm generally pleased with my decision-making abilities.	Not Satisfied 1 2 3 4 5	Satisfied 6 7 8 9 10
I tend to feel optimistic about most things.	Depressed 1 2 3 4 5	Optimistic 6 7 8 9 10
I generally consider myself a happy person.	Unhappy 1 2 3 4 5	Happy 6 7 8 9 10
I'm generally a stable, values-driven person.	Perplexed 1 2 3 4 5	Know What I Want 6 7 8 9 10
I feel committed to a meaningful purpose in life.	No Purpose 1 2 3 4 5	Commitment 6 7 8 9 10

RATE YOUR QUALITY OF LIFE

Scoring: Rate yourself on the 29 items. Add the total of your circled numbers and divide by 29 to get an average "balance" rating. Label yourself accordingly:

8–10: Calm and fulfilled
4–7: Coping but frustrated
1–3: Controlled and frantic

If your score falls in the 8–10 range, pat yourself on the back. In fact, you probably already feel pretty good about having time to take this test and reflect on how far you've come in feeling personal satisfaction with your life.

If your score falls in the 4–7 range, you should consider this a wake-up call. Look at the items on which you scored a 4 or 5, and begin there to identify specific changes you can make to loosen your life and move up a notch or two on the satisfaction scale.

If your score falls in the 1–3 range, you've probably panicked over losing the time to complete the questionnaire "with nothing to show for it" but despair. You need to take immediate steps to change the way you think about time and conduct your daily life and relationships. Otherwise, you stand a good chance of losing all that is important to you and coming to the end of your life with nothing to show for the journey.

CHANGE THE WAY YOU THINK ABOUT TIME

Time is the least thing we have of.—ERNEST HEMINGWAY

The question of life is not, How much time have we? The question is, What shall we do with it?—ANNA R. BROWN

Time, obviously, is relative. As someone has observed, "Two weeks on a vacation is not the same as two weeks on a diet."

The various clichés about time indicate its complexity: He's living on borrowed time. Time flies when you're having fun. We're working against time on this project. Time waits for no one. Time stands still for those in love. We arrived in the nick of time. It's time to stand up for what you think. It's high time she showed some interest. Time is money. He's having the time of his life. Let's find the time. We're losing time. She has too much time on her hands. You're wasting time. We're early enough to kill some time. Is it worth the time? Manage your time wisely. Take your time.

We all think about time differently. And our philosophies about time, aging, success, immortality, marinated mushrooms, and the day-to-day hustle show up in different ways in our lives. Our thoughts about time affect everything we do—our relationships, our work,

1

our successes. To be more specific, our concept of time determines whether we work late or go home to the kids. Eat instant oatmeal or cook an omelet. Wallpaper the closet or leave the shelves unfinished. Arrive early or late. Have surgery or accept the wrinkles. Cry or laugh. Ignore or help. Despair or hope.

How we allocate our minutes each day profoundly affects our career success, our charitable work, the quality of our personal lives, and the gift of ourselves that we leave behind for friends and family.

What is your personal philosophy of time? Write it out and think it over.

TIME FOR A CHECKUP

Do you generally equate time with money?

Do you typically find yourself "wasting" time?

Do you operate under the belief that you can always "correct for" misused time?

Do you plan your life around the clock?

Do you structure your life around your philosophy of time?

DEFINE SUCCESS IN YOUR OWN TERMS

The supposed great misery of our century is the lack of time.
—JOHN FOWLES

Do you confuse success with speed? Many people do. They buy fast cars, fast calls, fast computers, and fast food to accomplish more things in less time. And they confuse the exhilaration of the speed of the journey with the satisfaction upon arrival.

Through the years many people have defined themselves by their work. And they've come to enjoy the exhilaration of the speed of promotions, salary increases, and growing bank accounts. But since plateauing and massive layoffs have become common experiences, we have had to adjust to a slower speed of satisfaction. Those ideas of satisfaction were often holdovers of others' expectations—those of parents and society in general. Those who've plateaued on the job have broadened their journey and experienced satisfaction *as* they're traveling life's journey. They have learned they don't have to wait until the "end" for a successful "arrival."

Often we hear or read interviews with celebrities who say they're "surprised" by their success and recognition—that they never intended to be "successful" and set apart. That happens to many people—they just get caught up on a fast track mapped out by someone else and keep traveling that road without thought of where the destination leads.

More and more people nowadays are slowing down a bit to look out the window during their journey and asking if the destination "out there" is still worth passing up all the fantastic scenery and experiences along the route. Surveys of those starting their own businesses show that the most important reason for their entrepreneurial venture is having more control of their lives.

Gymnasts lose their balance when they take their eyes off the goal. Many of us have experienced the sensation of losing our balance in life because we still have our feet and bodies moving in one direction full speed ahead while our eyes have spotted a new destination.

The goal is to look in the same direction you're moving.

Label the pot of gold at the end of your rainbow. Here are some definitions of success I've collected through the years:

> "Success in Hollywood consists in having your name in the gossip columns and out of the phone book."

> "You're not successful till someone brags they sat beside you in grade school."

> "Some succeed by what they *know,* some by what they *do,* and a few by what they *are.*"

> "She has achieved success who has *lived* long, *laughed* often, and *loved* much."

> "Any person who is honest, fair, tolerant, charitable of others, and well-behaved is a success."

"Success is being the best in your chosen field."

"Success consists of doing common things of life uncommonly well."

"Success is serving your God and your fellow man."

Publisher and author Michael Korda says, "Success . . . is the distance between one's origins and one's final achievement."

"The good life is a process, not a state of being. It's a direction, not a destination."

"Success is having something to be enthusiastic about."

Thomas Wolfe defined it this way: "If a man has a talent and learns how to use it . . . he has gloriously succeeded and won a satisfaction and a triumph few men ever know."

Does this list generate some agreement or disagreement? Too many of us measure our success by what others have or haven't done. Too many of us have only a vague idea of what we ultimately want in life. And even if we can state it, we don't always translate that definition or belief to our daily work and decisions.

Reexamine your own idea of success. What are you chasing? What would you do with that dream if you ever caught it?

You personally have to select the way you'll measure your own success—the axiom you want to live by. Repeat it to yourself often. That definition or mission statement will help you translate success into everyday decisions. What job assignment you'll accept. How much overtime you'll work. How much time you'll spend with family. How much time you'll spend with friends. What time you'll devote to community projects. What time you'll spend on personal, self-improvement projects. Where you'll spend your money.

Your personal definition of success—if you have a firm grasp on it—will make many seemingly difficult decisions about time and activities much easier through the years. Your quality of life will depend on where you position the goal line.

TIME FOR A CHECKUP

Do you define success as a certain amount of money in the bank?

Do you define success by a job title?

Do you define success by awards for professional achievement?

Do you define success in terms of your relationships to others—family or friends?

Do you define success in commitment to a spiritual purpose?

Do you define success in terms of service to others?

Reflect on your life as a whole. What would you like others to write on your tombstone or say in their eulogy?

Do you routinely ask, "What does this activity contribute to my journey? Can I weed it out?"

ASSUME RESPONSIBILITY FOR HOW YOU USE YOUR TIME, YOUR LIFE, AND YOUR FUTURE

This life is a test; it is only a test. If it were a real life, you would receive instructions on where to go and what to do.—UNKNOWN

Time is neither our friend nor our enemy, it is something that gets measured out to us, to see what we will make of it.
—RICHARD G. BRILEY

Society has never respected those who are victims. Victims elicit empathy, sympathy, and pity—but not respect. When we find ourselves out of balance, the easiest thing to do about it is to begin blaming—other people at work who delegate meaningless tasks, family members at home "who don't pull their weight," circumstances of everyday life.

All these blaming tactics signal wrong thinking and bad habits. Clearly, some people must shoulder more than their fair share of difficult circumstances—those with a physical handicap or ongoing illness or those with heavy responsibilities for terminally ill family members. But for our lack of time, most of us create excuses for not changing attitudes, habits, or circumstances.

We blame traffic, the economy, government, the schools, peers, bosses, customers, or neighbors. We let others capture our time and then blame them for wrong priorities and poor results.

Alcoholics Anonymous insists that until someone can admit "I am an alcoholic," he or she cannot overcome the addiction to alcohol. The same is true with our pace of life. Until we admit that our decisions, actions, attitudes, and beliefs create the hectic pace, we cannot get off the merry-go-round.

TIME FOR A CHECKUP

Are you blaming others (boss, spouse, children, parents, friends) for the hectic pace of your life?

What are these people forcing on you that you have no option to control? (Accept these.)

What are these people forcing on you that you could control—if you had the courage to decide differently? (Change these.)

REALIGN YOUR
TIME WITH
YOUR VALUES

The greatest despair is not to become the person you were meant to be.—SÖREN KIERKEGAARD

I cannot afford to waste my time making money.—LOUIS AGASSIZ

Frustration about time and balance stems from the conflict between what we believe and value and what we actually do and have. For example:

We value time with our children, but we have to work long hours and travel in our job.

We enjoy spending time with our spouse, yet our weekends are filled with running errands in opposite directions just to get "caught up" and ready to go again the next week.

We value the emotional support from friends, but we never have time to carry on intimate conversations about real problems and issues in our lives or purposeful, fulfilling pursuits.

We value good health, but we can't find time to exercise. And we eat unbalanced meals that add calories without nutrition and, as a result, often feel tired and sick.

We believe serving God is a privilege and a duty, but we don't spend time in worship, and we don't get involved personally in meeting other people's needs as "God's hands on earth."

We value making a significant impact to our organization, but we have too many restrictions on the job to think creatively and take risks that might pay off.

We value leisure time to travel, yet we don't make enough money to pay for the travel that would fulfill us.

We value being socially accepted, but we don't have time to spend with friends or other professionals in social and civic get-togethers.

We value being successful in our job, but the job keeps changing before we can master what it's all about.

We value being recognized for accomplishments, but the company doesn't have a reward and recognition plan.

We value learning new skills, but the job doesn't offer professional development opportunities and training classes.

We value intellectual growth, but we don't have time to read, experiment with new ideas, and engage in meaningful conversations.

We value being appreciated by our spouse, but our spouse is too busy to notice the little things we do to help along the way.

We value teaching our children "about the world," but they're so busy in scheduled activities that we don't have time just to talk with them.

We value creativity, but our job allows only routine activities to maintain the status quo.

We believe that good citizens participate in government, yet we don't have time to study the various platforms and voting records of those running for office. So either we don't vote, or we make uninformed choices.

We value service to others, but we never volunteer time for charitable causes.

All these values come from our belief system developed throughout childhood and adulthood. After weeks, months, and years of not being able to live like you want to and have what you want, you feel like a traveler who packed for the wrong trip. All the want-to's are packed inside your head and heart, but you never get to "wear" them.

Instead of feeling angry and resentful, make up your mind to change what you have and what you do. You *can* make changes.

When my husband and I married, he valued his "stuff"—his furniture, his keepsakes from trips, his momentos from past jobs. And when we began the process of selling both houses and packing our "stuff" to move into one house, we had quite a struggle about what to throw away and what to save. I had a lamp; he had a lamp. My lamp was new; his lamp was old. Reason said to keep the new lamp and give away the old lamp. But reason wasn't the issue. After living alone for seventeen years, his stuff had become his life—a collection of who he was, his definition of himself. He had no children to call his own, and his physical possessions took on great value. But as his relationship with my children and family grew, he needed his stuff less and less to define him. The value he now places on stuff has decreased dramatically.

People who have successfully realigned time and activity with their values say they have accomplished or learned the following:

- They understand the true tradeoff between time and money.
- They are "doing" some of their dreams.
- They feel free.
- They feel relief from pressure.
- They feel guiltless.
- They have deeper relationships with spouse and children.
- They have more and deeper friendships.
- They live within their financial means and feel less financial stress.
- They have more "free time" to spend as they like.
- They have more time for self-development projects and learning.

Just as your car shimmies and shakes when its wheels are out of balance, your own mind and sense of well-being reacts when it's out of balance. Although not as easy as taking your car into the repair shop for a wheel realignment, you can realign yourself if you set your mind to do so.

TIME FOR A CHECKUP

Do you find yourself spending money on what you'd like to purchase or on what you feel you must buy?

Make a list of what you value in life (children? spouse? friends? charitable service? self-development opportunities? leisure time on hobbies?). Record how many hours you spend each week devoted to each item on the list.

DETERMINE THE LONG-TERM PAYOFF

Life is not dated merely by years. Events are sometimes the best calendars.—BENJAMIN DISRAELI

When you buy stocks, you expect to see a return on your money in a reasonable period. When you land a new job and work hard at it, you expect to be rewarded.

Investing in your children or in a charitable cause presents a problem. Unlike the stock market, neither character nor charity goes up or down overnight. You'll put in about 3285 hours reading bedtime stories, 72 hours walking through museums, 240 hours attending Little League games, 180 hours making medical visits, 36 hours applauding at school plays, 936 hours attending church or synagogue, 10,226 hours answering questions, 68 hours doling out discipline, and 3024 hours taking family outings before you'll see much of a trend at all.

In fact, you may not read your success as parents until you see the lives your kids lead as adults. You may not read your success with a community project or a social issue for decades.

Why don't we spend time on things that reflect our true values and have long-term payoff for us? One reason is that these long-term values and priorities are usually vague abstractions in our minds. They're not well-defined. For example, if I said I wanted to develop integrity, what would I do about that goal *today*? What are the concrete actions to take to develop integrity?

A second reason for delay is that long-term, high-priority activities never seem urgent. If you've been working on something for seven *years,* what difference does seven *days* make?

Third, long-term, high-priority activities are seldom critical to getting through the daily routine. They make up the "special" things that require effort and planning and forethought. They're easily postponed because they're so *important.*

Finally, long-term, high-priority activities don't get our attention because no one really has the authority to make us do these things. For example, who can make you be a better parent, a better spouse, a better financial manager, or a better planner? Those tasks are nobody's responsibility in our lives. As a result, these high-payoff activities and goals remain "out there" for another time.

Chances are you're going to be around for awhile. In 1894, the average life span in the United States was 49 years. Today, it is 72 for American men and 79 for American women. As you make decisions and choose where you'll spend your time, think about long-term payoff for what you're doing.

TIME FOR A CHECKUP

Do you have goals for longer than a year in the future?

If so, what specific activities did you do this past week to further each goal?

SET THE PACE ACCORDING TO THE PURPOSE

Time is nature's way of keeping everything from happening at once.—ANONYMOUS

All activities don't deserve your best efforts. Do you tend to eat your lunch with the same speed and urgency that you keyboard a million-dollar proposal? Excel where you should and don't bother where it doesn't count.

My small home town organized a fun run last year. My son and his friend home from college talked me into running with them. Why not? I jazzercize with my videotape. No big deal.

At the start of the race, my son and his friend jogged up beside me. Jeff said, "Mom, we're going to stay back with you." That was all I needed. "Stay *back* with me?" The fancy struck me that I might just stay *up* with them. So I gave him a nod and speeded up.

About five minutes into the race, the college friend said, "I think I'll run on ahead and see you two at the end." I glanced at my son who hadn't yet broken a sweat. I speeded up again. About ten minutes into the race, I realized I wasn't going to stay up with Jeff either. "Why don't you run on ahead too—I'll see you at the end."

"Oh, no, I'll stay back with you. We can talk."

As we turned the first corner I tried to glimpse the scattered bunches of runners behind me. Two, three, maybe four in view. Hmmm. At least I wasn't at the end. In fact, two teenaged girls in green windbreakers straggled behind me.

Into the third mile, I considered joining the walking group whose track intersected ours at that point. But just then Jeff said, "I'm surprised you're really doing this, Mom. It's so hot and everything." I kept moving.

Into the fourth mile, I pushed harder. I decided to let Jeff do the talking while I listened. My sides reminded me of my second-grade attack of appendicitis. Jeff obviously noticed the grimace. "Getting tired, Mom? It's not much farther."

"Me, tired? No. I'm fine."

"You're not talking."

"You talk. I'll listen."

"Okay, what do you want to listen about?"

"Why don't you go on ahead?"

His long legs beside me looked as though they were moving in slow motion. He shook his head, "No, it's okay. I'll just take it easy back here with you. No use pushing on my day off."

Fifth mile marker. "Mom, you want to stop?"

"Why do you keep asking me that?"

We finished still standing. Then I collapsed, every ounce of energy drained from my body. They blew a whistle and gathered us on the lawn for the trophy presentations. I could faintly hear the announcer begin with trophies for the "under ten years" category. Tuning in and out of the ceremonies, I faded into and out of consciousness. Then I heard them call my name.

My name? I sat up. Dianna Booher, third place in the forty to fifty category. Sure enough, I'd won third

place. With a nonchalant saunter to the edge of the crowd to claim my trophy, I felt a rush of excitement. Third place? Third place! Really. Not bad.

Then the announcer said, "Okay, fourth place winner. . . ." He fumbled with his piece of paper for a minute and then shook his head. "No, we don't have a fourth place in this category. There were only three runners in that age group. Let's move on to the last age group—fifty and above."

Third of three. I tried to make light of it to those seated around me in the grass. Inwardly, I began berating myself. Why hadn't I prepared for the run—got in better shape? If I'd have just run three miles for two weeks before, I could have done a lot better. Third of three.

"At least you finished," Jeff said. "Some people didn't finish."

Then his words began to ooze into my consciousness. He was right. Third of three. That meant only three of us had the courage to line up. In a matter of minutes, I traveled a long psychological distance—from thinking I could stay up with a twenty-two-year-old to feeling good about finishing near the bottom. All it took was just a slight trick of the mind.

Do you apply the same high standards of performance to *everything?* Do you clean the kitchen countertops every morning as if your realtor were showing your house to prospective buyers? Do you spend the same time planning the regular staff meeting agenda as you spend on a client meeting? Do you take as long to dress for a tennis match as you do for an evening on the town with friends?

Lack of talent or knowhow is *not* always the issue. It's attitude. It's pace. It's purpose. We know how to set a faster pace; the issue is with the *want* to and the *need* to.

What kind of pace are you setting for yourself? Which of your deadlines are self-imposed and which are real? Is it getting faster or slower? Does the pace match your purpose for the activity? Slow down for the fun runs. Dig in your heels for the major missions. And know the difference.

TIME FOR A CHECKUP

Do you recopy messy to-do lists so they look neater?

Do you let others impose standards of quality for projects at home—standards higher than what you think the work deserves?

Do you still feel as though you're getting a grade-school "report card" on all projects at work—and even ask for them from a boss?

Do you feel stress always to complete projects earlier than the deadlines given you by others?

Do you find it difficult to set priorities for tasks that all "need to be done at once"?

Do you frequently feel stressed when you see piles of to-dos on your desk—even if you have no particular deadline for them?

Do you purposefully complete work-related projects with your best efforts—even those less-important, routine things—as if your job depended on the perfection of each one?

STOP BEING SO IMPATIENT— *RIGHT NOW*

Folks used to be willing to wait patiently for a slow-moving stage coach, but now they kick like the dickens if they miss one revolution of a revolving door.—ED WYNN

Half our life is spent trying to find something to do with the time we have rushed through life trying to save.—WILL ROGERS

Whoever is out of patience is out of possession of his soul. Men must not turn into bees, and kill themselves in stinging others.—FRANCIS BACON

Impatience turns an argument into a fever, a fever to the plague, fear into despair, anger into rage, loss into madness, and sorrow to amazement.—JEREMY TAYLOR

At lunch recently the waiter stuck his head out from under the edge of our table, looking rather sheepish. He lifted my gray leather purse up and peered around the water glass. "Sorry. I just spilled salad dressing on your handbag." He waved the leather strap toward me so I could inspect the bag myself.

Sure enough, the bottom 2 inches of one side were about two shades darker gray than the rest. As I lifted the purse to look on the bottom, in addition to the splash of oil, I noticed a green dot of magic marker. No doubt, a remnant of some planning meeting in the conference room weeks . . . or years earlier.

The waiter called the manager from the back to make good. "Can you get it cleaned for me?" I asked him.

"No, but we'll be happy to have you take it somewhere and we'll reimburse you."

"But I need *you* to clean it."

"*We* can't clean it, ma'am."

One more thing for my to-do list! The next Saturday I was on a *mission:* Find a specialty cleaners. All the establishments I called cleaned leather—but not leather purses. The Town and Country Cleaners sent me to the Village Cleaners, who sent me to the MidCity Cleaners, who sent me to the Quick-Stop Cleaners. Finally, I walked into a dry-cleaners with a shoe repair shop under the same roof. The clerk on duty assured me without reservation, "Yes, we clean leather purses." Thrilled, I pushed the gray bag toward her and watched her write up the claim ticket.

"When can I pick it up?"

"It'll take a while. We send them out. The truck picks up only on Wednesdays. So they'll pick it up next Wednesday and then deliver it the following Wednesday. That okay?"

Out of habit, I protested. "Eleven days for cleaning?" She pushed the claim ticket toward me to fill in the name and address. At the next counter, a guy dashed in and shoved a stack of shirts toward the clerk. "How long will these take?"

"Will tomorrow be soon enough?"

"I guess it'll have to do."

I noted his rudeness. How could he wear all those shirts the next day anyway? But *I* needed my bag. His "how long will it take" reminded me of a scene a few months earlier when I'd gone to pick up my car after repairs for hail damage. A lady watched the wrecker pull her smashed Toyota into the repair shop and then asked, "How long will it take?"

The mechanic chuckled, shrugged at the heap of junk that would no doubt take miracles to restore, and winked. "Couple of hours, I imagine."

"Fine, thank you. Call me when it's ready," she responded on her way out. Obviously she hadn't even listened and assimilated his answer.

So why do we always ask? Why are we habitually impatient? With one-hour photos, one-hour eyeglasses, and mufflers while-you-wait, hurry has become a cultural habit.

I told the dry-cleaners clerk that the Wednesday after next would be fine for the purse. After all, the green magic marker had probably been on there for a while. They don't make that color anymore.

We're too impatient too often on too many unimportant things. To reduce stress, set your inner engine at a lower idling speed. When you catch yourself racing with your mind in overdrive, ask, "Why?"

Time for a Checkup

Do you walk up or down escalators?

Do you clear dishes from the table before others finish eating?

Do you eat standing up and fail to notice how your food tastes?

Do you unnecessarily pay for overnight, "rush" service at the tailor's, cleaners, print shop?

Do you shuffle and fidget when standing in lines at the grocery store or bank—even when you're not particularly facing a deadline?

Do you often say "hurry" to others—your kids, your spouse, your coworkers?

Do you strum your fingers when you're left sitting idle for a few minutes?

Do you frequently ask for an earlier appointment when your beautician or barber tells you their first available appointment time?

Do you routinely drive over the speed limit?

Do you catch yourself telling service people to "keep the change" simply because you don't want to wait rather than because they gave good service?

RID YOURSELF OF THE TIMEKEEPERS IN YOUR LIFE

Modern man thinks he loses something—time—when he does not do things quickly, yet he does not know what to do with the time he gains—except kill it.—ERICH FROMM

Experience has taught me this, that we undo ourselves by impatience.—MICHEL EYQUEM DE MINTING

You know who these people are. A customer who keeps calling you every few days to ask how you're coming on the project not due for another three months. A boss who asks you to account for every moment of your day. A spouse who reminds you of how long it takes you to complete any given chore. A child who follows you around the house, asking, "Is it time to go yet?" A relative who phones to ask if you've made your plans for the holidays yet—11 months early?

These timekeepers may have perfectly legitimate reasons for reminding you of the time and of caring about the time for themselves. But if these frequent reminders, questions, and probes make you feel uncomfortable or make you feel that you're always behind, try your best to shut them out.

How? Keep the ball in your court, with statements such as these: "I'll be in touch at the end of next month to give you an update on the project." "I'll let you know when I'm ready to do X." "I'll make myself a calendar note to call you the minute I've made a decision about the holidays."

If this tactic doesn't work with certain individuals, explain outright that you have your own clock or calendar to keep track of the time and don't need or appreciate reminders. Do, however, keep your word about keeping others updated, or you will lose credibility for the next occasion—as well as become someone's irritant.

TIME FOR A CHECKUP

Do you keep others informed about your plans when what you do may affect their own scheduling or activities?

Can others depend on your sense of time?

Are you punctual for activities?

Do you routinely meet project deadlines without external nudging?

DROP PERFECTIONISM AS A HABIT

The difference between "good enough" and "perfect" is a logarithmic increase in effort.—OTIS BAUGHMAN, M.D.

So rather than criticizing and resenting the imperfect system, I practice this philosophy: It is better to strike a straight blow with a crooked stick than spend my whole life trying to straighten the darn thing out.—KEN BLANCHARD, WILLIAM ONCKEN, AND HAL BURROWS

A good plan today is better than a perfect plan tomorrow.
—PATTON'S LAW

Mediocrity has gotten a bad name. All those sports figures labeled mediocre may still enjoy being grouped with the greats. Mediocrity is in itself a decision about priorities. All things don't deserve our best efforts. Become your own best judge about which areas or issues you can accept less-than-perfect performance.

Perfectionism reduces productivity. Because our company teaches communication workshops to corporate clients (including business and technical writing), it's very difficult to see a typo, a misspelled word, or an awkward grammatical construction without stopping to correct it. But when my assistant inputs research notes in my database, typing about 100 words a minute, she's going to have a few typos and less-than-polished sentences. But what's the point in correcting these errors when no one will read the notes but me? When I insisted that my assistant *not* slow down to correct such mistakes, her data entry speed took a quantum leap.

Where are you tempted to waste time doing a perfect job when only a mediocre one will do? Redrafting documents? Cleaning out your desk? Making dinner from "scratch"? Refusing to chart the performance of one mutual fund until you have time to graph them all? Waiting to clean out the hall closet until you have time to advertise and hold a garage sale? Refusing to delegate a project to someone who won't do a task as well as you would do it yourself? Failing to buy someone a gift because you couldn't decide on the *perfect* gift?

If you find yourself without choice in such matters, then perfectionism has become a compulsion. Cut loose.

Time for a Checkup

Do you have a reputation at work or home as someone difficult to please?

Do people frequently tell you that you "overdo it"?

Do you hesitate to try a new sport because you're afraid you won't play well?

Does not doing well at a game put you in a bad mood?

Do you look for shortcuts in doing chores (repairs, cooking, shopping, cleaning, routine work projects)? Good—find more of them.

EVALUATE YOUR MINUTES IN MONETARY STANDARDS AND DECIDE WHAT'S WORTH PAYING FOR

You don't really pay for things with money. You pay for them with time.—UNKNOWN

I want money in order to buy the time to get things that money will not buy.—CARL SANDBURG

Our costliest expenditure is time.—THEOPHRASTUS

Time is everything. Anything you want, anything you can accomplish—pleasure, success, fortune—is measured in time.
—JOYCE HALL

Your work year contains approximately 2000 hours. Divide your salary and benefits by 2000 hours for a rough estimate of the worth of your *work* time. (*Don't*, however, consider this dollar figure to be the actual worth of your time altogether—but more about that in later discussions.) Let's say you're making $60,000 per year. That means your work hours are worth $30 each. Does it make sense to mow your own lawn if you could hire it done for $15 an hour? That depends. If you're in business for yourself or on commission and if not mowing your own lawn would enable you to spend two more hours on the telephone selling widgets, then your $30 investment on a lawn service would net you $60 worth of commissions.

But there's more to the equation than that simple one. If you hire someone to mow your lawn for $30 and still knock off the phone work two hours early, then you've lost money on the transaction. Or, if you enjoy the outdoor work on the lawn and feel the break rejuvenates you for the shorter day of work, you're still ahead by mowing your own lawn.

Ours has become a service economy. We pay for someone else to cook our food, do our laundry, clean our houses, prepare our taxes, perm our hair, shop for our gifts, repair our appliances, and maintain our sports equipment.

The point is this: Do a true evaluation before you trade money for services. If you're running yourself crazy doing things that you could hire done, pay someone else for these personal services. But if the amount of money you pay for services is forcing you to work longer hours to cover the expense, think again. Is the tail wagging the dog?

TIME FOR A CHECKUP

Are you losing hours of work time and creating stress for yourself by trying to do tasks and errands that are relatively inexpensive to buy?

What services are you now paying for that you'd enjoy doing for yourself—if you had the time?

BE WARY OF HIGH-TECH, TIME-SAVING DEVICES

The clock, not the steam engine, is the key machine of the modern industrial age.—LEWIS MUMFORD

High-tech may mean high-time.

Not too long ago we purchased network software in the office to keep ourselves organized—a calendar and scheduling package. Although it's clearly an answer to scheduling client workshops and convention speeches and informing all others about my whereabouts on any given day, it's certainly more time-consuming to enter daily reminders and to-dos on the computer than on a paper calendar.

Before buying any "time-saving" gadget, consider the hidden investment of time in its use: time to select and purchase the appropriate item, time to learn how to operate it, time to set it up and store it and secure it, time to refurbish or repair it, time to insure it and replace it.

Low-tech items like the pencil, broom, razor blade, spoon, and bucket can be real timesavers themselves. Before making a major purchase of some time-saving device, ask a user how much time he or she has spent upfront on the item before it increased productivity? Consider how frequently you'll use the gadget to complete a certain task. Then evalute the total time investment per use of the gadget. Does your need of the item justify that investment of time over the long haul?

Time for a Checkup

Are you using high-tech at the office when low-tech is just as quick and competent?

Are you using high-tech at home when low-tech works just as well and just as quickly?

Can you "undo" such purchases and stop the expenditure of time and money in maintaining and insuring?

SET GOALS,
THEN RAISE AND
LOWER THE BAR

*If you want something to happen, make a space for it. . . .
Practically all goals tarnish with time if not renewed in some
way.*—DAVID CAMPBELL, PH.D.

Since childhood, external forces and circumstances have compelled us toward goals. As a young person, we have many goals set before us: finish high school, finish college, find a marriage partner, find a job. Then as a newlywed and new employee, we have other goals: make a good impression, get a promotion, build a solid marriage, raise well-adjusted children, save for a home or children's education or retirement, make a difference in the world, build a community.

But about mid-life, goals get fuzzy. You may question the worthiness of a specific goal. James Ogilvy, in his book *Living Without Goals,* points out that life is full of things that prepare you for a life of perpetual preparation for life. Life becomes a "curriculum." That summation is true in two situations: when we let others set our goals and when we neglect goals in some areas of our life.

Goals should run the gamut of life: health and fitness goals, relationship goals, spiritual goals, career goals, financial goals, social goals, political goals, personal growth goals. The biggest goal I ever set for myself was to become a full-time writer. At that early stage of my life, I didn't even know what was involved. My idea was to set a typewriter in the corner of the bedroom, type out my novel while the kids took a nap, send off the manuscript, and then wait for the movie version to come out.

And I don't have to tell you that if I had stopped there, that would still be a "goal" rather than a job. For you to reach goals successfully, you must

- Be specific.
- Add a deadline.
- Develop an action plan.
- Chart your progress.

Back to my goal as full-time writer. You'll notice that my goal wasn't "to find a job where I can be creative." Too vague. There are no ads in the classifieds listed as "creative" jobs.

Then came the deadline. I gave myself one full year after quitting my full-time teaching job. If I hadn't made some headway by the start of the next school year, then I had decided that I'd have to return to teaching and a steady salary.

Next came the action plan. I couldn't afford to go back to school full-time at that point in my life, so my plan of action was simple—to go to the library and check out every book on writing on the shelf—from writing greeting card verses to the romance novel to the technical journal article.

Finally, I had to chart my progress. That meant setting intermediate, daily, and weekly goals like sending out ten query letters to editors per week for how-to articles and writing at least one short story per week.

If we're not making progress toward our goals, then something's wrong. Our goals need to be reexamined. Don't mistake worthy goals for only those that require action and effort. Some goals may require no action or effort—such as to reduce your workweek by five hours over the next year or to spend less time managing your investments or to take three extra days of vacation.

Are your own goals specific? What is your real commitment to each goal? Is the goal realistic? Is the goal timely? Do you have realistic deadlines to accomplish each? Your answer to these questions may lead you to modify or replace a goal.

After you set a goal, go for it:

- Prepare.
- Take action toward the goal.
- Revise time frames and tactics as necessary.
- Adapt your goals to fit those goals of significant others in your life.
- Assume responsibility for your progress or lack of progress.
- Raise or lower the bar on the goal, as you grow in self-knowledge.

Are you managing your life by objectives, or just letting it "happen"? Are you pleased with the results?

TIME FOR A CHECKUP

What are your personal goals? Are they specific?
Do you have deadlines? What are your action plans?

What are your family goals? Are they specific?
Do you have deadlines? What are your action plans?

What are your career goals? Are they specific?
Do you have deadlines? What are your action plans?

What are your financial goals? Are they specific?
Do you have deadlines? What are your action plans?

What are your spiritual goals? Are they specific?
Do you have deadlines? What are your action plans?

DON'T LIVE TO ACCOMPLISH GOALS—LIVE IN THE PRESENT

Nothing should be prized more highly than the value of each day.—GOETHE

Real generosity toward the future lies in giving all to the present.—ALBERT CAMUS, FROM THE REBEL

Our main task is not to see what lies dimly perceived in the future, but to do the thing which lies immediately at hand.—THOMAS CARLYLE

Have you ever known people who have been preparing to live—all their life? They've spent years in school. They've been saving almost every penny for a down payment on something. They've been going to work sick because they're saving their sick leave and vacation days until they "need" them.

In past decades self-worth was tied to tangibles. People performed hard labor and received cash in their hands. Cash bought the necessities of life and, if possible, even luxuries. Today, our work is much less tangible. How do you explain the job of a PR agent, a lawyer, a stockbroker, a department director in tangible outputs? In our white-collar, information-based economy, an individual's self-worth is often tied to achievements rather than possessions.

How does one achieve? Set and accomplish goals—many of them, intangible goals. As a result, people sometimes fall over the edge of now into the future. Preparation, forethought, and planning are admirable—unless they overshadow the present and prevent us from enjoying every day.

Time for a Checkup

Do you make to-do lists every day of your life and transfer what you didn't get done today onto tomorrow's list?

Do you ever live a week without a list?

When is the last time you made an impromptu decision and spent three hours on an unscheduled, pleasurable activity—just because?

Have you enjoyed today as much as you plan to enjoy next year or the next decade?

RID YOURSELF OF PERFORMANCE JITTERS

BECOME EMPLOYABLE FOR A LIFETIME

One realizes the full importance of time only when there is little of it left. Every man's greatest capital asset is his unexpired years of productive life.—P. W. LITCHFIELD

Much of our feeling of imbalance comes from working long hours—against our will and druthers. Ask many people why they do it, and you'll hear fear and uncertainty about the security of their jobs. According to the latest *Employment and Earnings* journal of the U.S. Department of Labor, over 3 million people were laid off last year. After such massive layoffs associated with right-sizing and reengineering of corporate America, job security and lifetime employment with one company are things of the past.

To add to that stress of insecurity, many organizations are ushering in competition once again. For all the talk of collaboration, teamwork, and team incentives, competition has reared its head in the forced rankings of performance—of and by peers. Organizations now base raises on the job rankings—with the top fraction receiving raises and the bottom fraction fearing they'll be the first to be laid off in times of downturns. For those who get to keep their jobs, companies have revamped their compensation packages to incorporate the concept of skill-based pay.

So workers are putting in longer hours to show their commitment to their tasks and to pass muster with their peers. And add to this stress the stress of not even being sure you understand what your job is. Because of my consulting and speaking roles, I'm often in and out of large corporations, meeting lots of different people. In moments of idle chit-chat, when I ask name, department, title, or job responsibilities, I'm frequently hearing responses like this one from a professional at a large oil company in Houston: "I don't have a title yet; my job is to figure out my job."

If you have anxiety about your own job, do a quick analysis. What are you paid to do? What are two or three key objectives your supervisor expects you to accomplish? How much of your time do you devote to these two or three objectives? What other time-consuming things are keeping you from accomplishing these objectives? Find ways to cut through these peripheral tasks by delegating them, eliminating them, or streamlining them.

To reduce the remaining stress in such a situation, you have to undergird your security by knowing you're employable for a lifetime. Take every opportunity you can to attend training classes and fine-tune your skills so that you have an arsenal of skills at your disposal for new jobs with your current employer or skills that will make you attractive to a new employer.

Be responsible for your own ongoing learning.

TIME FOR A CHECKUP

What job skills need to be updated?

What plans do you have for self-study (books, tapes, CD-ROM courses) to enhance general professional skills such as writing, making oral presentations, listening, communicating one-on-one, resolving conflict, negotiating, persuading, leading and participating in meetings?

BECOME MORE SELECTIVE ABOUT YOUR INTAKE OF INFORMATION AND NEWS

A learned blockhead is a greater blockhead than an ignorant one.—BENJAMIN FRANKLIN

News is the same thing happening everyday to different people.—ANONYMOUS

In 1932 *Time* magazine did two stories on the kidnapping of the Lindbergh baby. In 1994 to 1995, the magazine ran twenty-nine articles on the O. J. Simpson trial.

If you're the typical American, you hear hours of radio and TV broadcasts daily, read at least one newspaper a day, and thumb through several magazines a month. That's a flood of free-floating information.

Add to that the 50,000 to 55,000 books published annually in the United States alone. It has been estimated that the world's greatest libraries are doubling in size every fourteen years. According to researchers Wilbur Shramm and William Porter, several libraries in the world have inventories of over 8 million books each.

And by their count, approximately 9600 different periodicals are published in the United States each year.

That will give you some idea of how much information we have bombarding us every waking moment. And that doesn't even account for the information we take in by conversation, computer, fax, phone, or mail.

Our brains can't possibly process all that information. We must filter it so we can focus on things that are useful, applicable, and of interest to us specifically and individually.

Particularly bad news blaring at us from the TV and radio or glaring from the newspaper can warp our sense of the world and create free-floating anxiety and even depression.

I've discovered that it's possible—even preferable—to be a reasonably informed, intelligent individual without taking a daily dose of the news. Although once an addict of dailies and weeklies, I'm on my way to being cured of information overload. When I started traveling heavily with my job about twelve years ago, I refused to stop the newspaper while away. Instead, upon my return, I would faithfully skim each edition for editorials, features, or reviews I may have missed while on the road with unfamiliar sources. Of course, on the hard-news sagas of ongoing situations and issues, I'd play catch-up once at home by starting with the latest issue of the paper and read backward, knowing I was getting the final word on each story and skipping the in-between patter written before the final resolution.

Then it dawned on me: If I could read only the final installment of each ongoing political issue, social issue, or scandal after traveling, why waste time reading the middle trivia altogether? Why not just skip the articles dealing with "will he or won't he," "what if and what if not," "which version will get through Congress and which won't," and instead wait for the *final* resolution?

On the few conversational occasions when I've been lost with regard to some news event, I've simply admitted, "I'm sorry, but I haven't been following that story/issue/scandal," and then listened as the other person filled me in for about sixty seconds about something that might have wasted hours of my reading time.

Instead of a negative-news intake valve, use TV as a self-development tool by watching networks like TPN (The Peoples Network), with its total programming on self-development topics.

But the bigger issue here is psychic relief. We've used technology and travel to create a fog of unreality about what's real and what's not. We've become voyeurs on the world and blind to our own needs.

My philosophy: filter the general deluge of information. Read specifically. Don't read it until you need to use it. Then know where to find it.

TIME FOR A CHECKUP

How many newspapers do you read daily?

How many news broadcasts do you hear daily?

Do you ever feel sad or depressed about the hopelessness of the world's situation, as depicted in the news?

How many professional and business journals do you read monthly? How many articles have significantly contributed to your professional growth?

PLAN OR PLUMMET

If I had eight hours to chop down a tree, I'd spend six hours sharpening my ax.—ABRAHAM LINCOLN

There's never time to do it right, but always time to do it over.
—JOHN MESKIMEN

Successful *companies* have elaborate plans. Successful *individuals* have elaborate plans. That's true for writing a book, running a business, teaching a course, or running weekend errands.

When I write the typical book—if there is such a thing—I may spend 12 months researching, two weeks outlining it, and only two to ten days doing the actual writing. Even Saturday morning errands go faster with a plan drawn up before you get in the car.

Some people resist planning because they think it takes the spontaneity out of whatever it is they're doing. That's nonsense. That's like saying that if you stop by the bank and get some cash, you'll take the fun out of dining and the theater later. Or, if you read a few consumer reports, glance through a few auto manufacturers booklets, and attend an auto show that you'll destroy the thrill of buying a new car.

Others reject the idea of planning because they say planning takes too much time. Experience shows just the opposite. When you consider all the "go rounds" and unanticipated delays caused by failure to plan, *not* planning is what costs too much time.

Your plan for any given project or timeframe can be simple. You can plan by the month or year. By the project. Even by the day.

Plan for the long term. What new training will you need? Where can you get it? What financing do you need? Where should you live? Who should you know? What experiences should you have?

Plan for the short term. Don't assume that since few days are typical, you can't plan for the everyday happenings. Plan for the routine, and then plan for the typical atypical happenings.

Set deadlines and measurements for all you plan. Then stick to them. Decide how much time, money, or stress a project is worth. If it costs more, put an end to it. Use the fish-or-cut-bait principle to plan the time you'll commit to any one task or project.

Be careful, of course, that your time horizon for planning is long enough. Many people like to plan for things about which they don't have to project much into the future. Instead, as you plan, consider the consequences of a decision, action, or event by casting your sights a little further into the future.

Review your long-term and short-term objectives routinely. Break the big tasks into doable steps. Schedule the tasks in a realistic way—within the available time in any given day, week, or month. Anticipate setbacks and obstacles along the way and plan what you'll do to alter your course.

But do plan.

TIME FOR A CHECKUP

Do you plan routinely—or only when you are already in a big time crunch?

How far ahead do you plan for important events?

Do you often operate in crisis mode because of failure to plan far enough in advance?

CLUTTER YOUR TO-DO LIST, NOT YOUR MIND

Time flies. It's up to you to be the navigator.—ROBERT ORBEN

Your mind can hold only about seven chunks of information at once. Why push your luck? Why try to remember what you have to do, think about, or solve when you can download the pressure onto paper?

Do you frequently have flashes of brilliance when you're in the shower, out for a walk, or driving down the freeway? Write them down immediately rather than juggle them in your mind—a waste of energy, not to mention the chance for forgetting altogether.

Just because you make a to-do list doesn't mean that you must stick to it. In route to completion, you may decide that some tasks can be left undone without harm. In fact, before you start each new task, ask yourself what would happen if you left it undone. If you can accept the consequences, cross the item off your list without guilt.

But do use paper for this indecision—not your mind. *I should. . . . Maybe I shouldn't. . . . Maybe I can. . . . Maybe I can't. . . .* Thinking about it creates anxiety and frustration that breaks your concentration. Each time you change your mind, change your list. Paper is cheap; your mind isn't.

Those who make lists stay on target and save time between tasks and ideas without wondering what comes next. Those who don't make lists are at the mercy of mishaps, memory, and mediocrity.

TIME FOR A CHECKUP

Do you routinely make notes to yourself of important information, or just when your mind feels overwhelmed?

Are you a slave to your list? (Treat the list as a crutch, not a commandment.)

USE THE
2 × 2 × 2 RULE

Arranged time is the surest mark of a well-arranged mind.
—Anonymous

Use the 2 × 2 × 2 rule (two-hour, two-day, two-week rule) to eliminate desk stress. This principle is particularly helpful when you return to the office after a long absence and find a mountain of paperwork.

Sort with this rule in mind:

Two-minute (or less) tasks due in two hours or less. What must I do immediately—within a couple of hours? Things like urgent calls and notes from your staff who're waiting on a simple answer before they can take further action on a project. All those items go in the two-hour pile, each to be handled in about two minutes or less.

Two-hour (or less) tasks due in two days or less. Sort into the two-day pile things that can wait only a couple of days and that will take longer than a couple of minutes but not more than two hours. Tasks like answering a client's letter. The agenda for a seminar. Collecting information for a report.

Two-day (or more) tasks that can wait for two weeks. In the final pile—the two-week pile—sort projects that will take you longer than two hours to complete and for which you have at least two weeks before the deadline. A report to write. An outline for an upcoming presentation.

Two hours. Two days. Two weeks. After you have those three priority piles, work them. Put the two-week items off to the side (preferably in the files), out of your work space, with a reminder note on your calendar to come back to them. Clip through the two-minute/two-hour pile quickly; that'll build your momentum and a sense of accomplishment. Then work your way through the two-hour/two-day pile of short, but urgent projects with maximum concentration and focus.

Time for a Checkup

Do you let paperwork pile up until you become distressed just looking at it?

Do you receive a lot of "reminders" from others, requesting paperwork still on your desk?

Do you feel as though you're "darting" from a small project to a major project with little forethought?

Do you find it difficult to concentrate on a major task because "little things" keep nagging at you from left field?

Are you ever tempted to stop the major project to do "a few little things" and then fail to find time to return to the major project?

ORGANIZE THINGS SO YOU CAN FIND THEM

Let all things be done decently and in order.—1 CORINTHIANS 14:40

Do you spend precious minutes looking for things around the house and at the office? Do you buy things you already have because you can't find what you've already bought? In a family emergency, could someone find all the paperwork they need to keep your household, finances, or office running without you? Does this bother you?

Looking at an overflowing desk piled high with paper distresses most people. That scene represents a race track with incoming communication having lapped the field several times ahead of you.

People do rationalize about it with comments such as, "Actually, I know where everything is." "Disorganization is the sign of a creative mind." "Look how busy I am and how much I have to handle." "I know it's here—somewhere."

If paper piles don't bother you—or the people who must interact with you on various projects—then by all means forget this principle. However, if you have to admit that the disorganization causes you mental stress and saps precious time that you'd rather spend with your family, then organization is worth your attention.

When paper lands on your desk, you can do one of five things with it:

- Discard it.
- Do it.
- Delegate it.
- Dump it in a temporary follow-up file.
- Dump it in a permanent file.

If you don't do one of these things with it, you have a decision-making problem, not an organization problem at hand.

The old rule of "handle paper only once" isn't always appropriate; you cannot always complete a project or communication with one reading. You may have to wait for more information or make a phone call to get agreement from someone else or think over the situation. *But you can move the action forward by one step with each handling.* That is, if you can't immediately discard it, do it, or delegate it, and you're forced to put it in a temporary follow-up file, then at least note on the top of that paper what the next step is and what you're waiting for.

For example, stick a note on the front that says, "Decide whether to attend this meeting after talking to Joe about X." Then when you come to that piece of paper again in your follow-up stack, you'll not have to read it and rethink the situation. Instead, you can take the next action immediately.

So how do you begin to get organized? You need a place to sort. Clear a spot to begin the clean-up operation and sort the piles as mentioned in the 2 × 2 × 2 chapter. Then leave a clean space on your desk to work on each project at hand.

The primary rule of staying organized is *to have a place for everything*. An organized system/space is easier to *maintain* than to create. So you may want to call in an organization expert to help you set up your office and then just maintain what he or she sets up for you. If you want to attempt the project yourself, here are some questions that will serve as a checklist of what needs to find a home somewhere:

Do you have an extra set of keys for your vehicles, home, and possessions located for easy access by you or others in case of emergency?

Do you have a list of credit card numbers and phone numbers to call in case your cards are lost or stolen?

Do you have warranties, receipts, and instructions for major appliances and equipment located in one place for easy access?

Do you have a list of all valuables (their original purchase amount and date and their serial numbers) for insurance purposes in case of loss?

Do you have all significant dates marked on one calendar (birthdays, anniversaries, and annual social and professional events)?

Do you have items stored in your car for road emergencies—flashlight, jumper cables, extra tires, blankets?

Do you have fire extinguishers and alarms in your home and office?

Do you have an up-to-date financial file and power-of-attorney, listing all your account numbers and financial institutions so that someone else could handle your affairs in case of emergency?

When you unload your desk and organize your space and life, your mind will feel lighter.

TIME FOR A CHECKUP

Do you frequently come across a piece of paper on your desk that you had completely forgotten about?

Do you frequently waste five minutes looking for something (or having an assistant look) because you can't remember what you did with it?

Do you frequently receive "follow-up" memos and calls for information/approvals/input requested earlier— while the original request is still on your desk?

Do you have a reputation (get teased) for having a messy desk or office?

Do coworkers put things in your hands or in your chair or stick notes on your computer screen or door so you won't "miss" them rather than put them in your overflowing in-box or on your desk?

When you want to get serious work done, do you have to clean off a place to work or find a different office or table?

CUT THE CLUTTER

Set thine house in order.—ISAIAH 38:1

When my husband and I married and combined our households, we discovered that he (living alone for seventeen years) had more stuff stored in his house than all three people in my household put together—way, way more. Here are the explanations behind the various items he felt worthy of packing, moving, and finding a new home for (and my ready responses):

- "I paid good money for that. Do you know how much it would cost to replace that?" (My response: "Why would you want to replace it if you don't use it?")

- "C. Jane gave that to me when I was living in El Paso." (My response: "Do you need this to remember your sister and El Paso? Will they care that you no longer have it?")

- "We might need that." (My response: "When? For what? Couldn't we buy another one then? If we needed it someday, we wouldn't be able to find this one in less than a three-hour search. And besides that, it's broken.")

- "That magazine's got some good information in there— and even a map." (My response: "What article/information/map? Let's clip it. For which project did you need it? Is it the only map of that location? If you need it someday, would you know where to find it—quickly?")

■ "This will be a collector's piece someday." (My response: "Will we live that long? Do you want to give it to the kids to see if they live that long?")

■ "That blazer will come back in style—just you wait." (My response: "Are you kidding? The style may come back, but the length or sleeve cut or fabric or color won't be right. Designers aren't that accommodating.")

■ "That's still like brand new. It's never been used." (My response: "So why keep something you haven't and won't use? Who do we know to give it to?" "How about the church mission?")

■ "That belongs to Cary." (My response: "Can we call him and see if he wants it back? If not, ask him what he suggests we do with it.")

■ "All that needs is a new switch and it'll work as good as new." (My response: "Okay, so do you want to take it and get it repaired? Or, if you want to fix it, how about this weekend?")

■ "That's a souvenir from my Disney trip." (My response: "So do you want to play with it now, or look at it, or give it to your nieces and nephews? Or, dust it weekly?")

■ "That's not mine—I don't know where that came from." (My response: "Great. If we throw it away, nobody will miss it.")

Our solution? A gradual dump. We packed up what he couldn't bear to discard at that moment and agreed to leave it in the attic for the year we intended to live in a rental house while the new one was being built. If he hadn't "needed" the item in a year, it was up for a second discussion.

Some of those items are still packed away in boxes and will be up for a third discussion when we move again next month. (But at least they're not cluttering up living space.)

Here are the cluttering culprits in most households: Out-of-date catalogs. Out-of-date magazines and journals. Textbooks and school annuals. Greeting cards from years past. Instruction booklets/receipts for items already discarded. Photographs of people you don't recognize, along with negatives and double prints from every vacation. Clothes that are out of style, worn out, inappropriate for the climate, or don't fit. Uniforms from occupations or hobbies long past. Kitchen gizmos that you don't use. Broken appliances. Old files of outdated insurance policies, vehicle registrations, bank reconciliation statements, investments you no longer have and the like. Knickknacks that collect dust. Sports and hobby equipment for sports you don't play and hobbies you no longer have.

So what's the problem in keeping all this clutter? It takes up space you could be living in. And you're paying to insure, heat, cool, and light the space. Occasionally, you have to spray it for rodents/insects, move it, or clean it to put in a garage sale.

If you tend to have clutter creep in your living space, try this suggestion: Keep a clutter control corner/cubicle for each room. Designate that one spot for all the items that are in transition—they're temporary but you can't bear to part with them yet or decide where to put them permanently. That way, when something's missing, you know which corner or box to search. Also, when visitors arrive, straightening (or hiding) one cluttered corner/box is better than trying to restore the whole room to order.

To get off junk mail lists and prevent those catalogs, gadgets, or other tempting invitations from arriving at your door, write Mail Preference Service, Direct Marketing Association, 11 West 42d Street, P.O. Box 3861, New York, NY 10163-3861. Request that your name be removed from mailing lists sold from company to company. Also, when you do order something or respond to an invitation through the mail, request that that company not add your name to their mailing list and that they not sell it.

If you find yourself surrounded by clutter—and are tempted to keep it indefinitely—ask: If I wanted this someday, would I remember that I have it? Would I know where to find it immediately? Would I want to take the time to find it (clean it up, repair it) for use? Could I find or buy another one with less effort and time?

TIME FOR A CHECKUP

Do you really want to pay utility bills, insurance costs, construction costs, or rent for all you have stored?

Do others in your life agree with your explanations and reasons for keeping items?

What's your system for finding things you've stored away?

EQUIP MULTIPLE PLACES OF EXISTENCE

*Have a place for everything and keep the things somewhere else.
That is not advice, it is merely custom.*—MARK TWAIN

Wherever you need to do work, have there what you need—paper, pen, stamps, stationery, stapler and extra staples, rubber bands, binder clips, phone, calculator, computer, food. Wherever you get caught, you can get a few things done . . . completely.

There's nothing more exasperating than having nine projects *almost* finished—except that you need to make a copy of this item, need to sign that contract in black ink, need a stamp to mail the payment, or have to add the expense column and don't have a calculator handy. With the routine tools at hand, you can *finish* all these petty little projects while you're waiting in the car, in the line, in the lobby.

Then get a transport system for what you have to carry back and forth. (You can now buy car caddies—partitioned trays for all your gadgets.) Sorting and packing and then resorting and repacking into your briefcase can be a time-consuming chore. If you have several continuing projects, then have a bag, case, or binder for each. In my case, I have a satchel for all my financial papers, so when I get ready to pay bills and reconcile bank statements, I can just grab that bag and take it to my computer. I have a "research" catalog case, where I keep files of ongoing book research and all sorts of related items such as interlibrary loan forms and library information sheets. I have a binder with Bible study materials and class roster for my weekly sessions with couples. Then I have the typical briefcase for everyday papers relating to current projects that I take back and forth from home to office.

The transport system (items packed separately in separate cases) saves approximately an hour a week of resorting—and most important, it ensures that I show up somewhere with all I need.

TIME FOR A CHECKUP

Do you miss opportunities to get a few little things done while unexpectedly waiting because you don't have what you need at hand?

Do you have scissors, stapler, stamps, paperclips, notepad, calculator in your car, office, home office, school nook, or cubicle?

READ FASTER AND WITH PURPOSE

We are what we read.—RICHARD SAUL WURMAN

We are creating and using up ideas and images at a faster and faster pace. Knowledge, like people, places, things, and organizational forms, is becoming disposable.—ALVIN TOFFLER

The typical office manager sends or receives an average of 49 faxes per day, at a length of 5 pages each. There are between 50,000 and 55,000 *new* books published each year in the United States. According to the latest *Gale Directory,* more than 38,000 newspapers, journals and magazines are published to keep you up to date on current events, culture, or career.

You can't keep up. The solution to feeling less bombarded and behind is to read faster and with purpose.

First, read only what's of interest to you. You'd never think of letting someone barge into your office or your home without an appointment. But we often let mail and freebie magazines or newsletters nag us to be read. If you can't see an immediate use for it, if you didn't subscribe to it, if you didn't request it, if you don't know why you got it, discard it without reading it.

Second, if you do have interest in reading something, read with a purpose and a plan. How are you going to use the information? Can you get the gist of what you want to know by reading the blurbs, summary, headline, headings, graphics, and accompanying captions?

If you need more, read the first sentence of each paragraph and the bulleted lists. If you need still more, skim for statistics, names, sites, projects and follow-up information.

If you're reading because you need information (as opposed to reading for pleasure), then read as little as possible, with a purpose at hand, and then move on. With the time saved, read more things for which you have stronger interest and bigger payoff.

TIME FOR A CHECKUP

Does your stack of professional journals contain issues or articles at least six months old?

Do stacks of freebie newsletters, catalogs, and magazines "nag" you?

USE THE TELEPHONE AS A TOOL, NOT A TIME TRIFLER

Just because your voice reaches halfway around the world does-n't mean you are wiser than when it reached only to the end of the bar.—EDWARD R. MURROW

A teenage girl reports that she's been trying to run away from home for several months—but every time she gets to the front door the phone rings.—ANONYMOUS

Telephone technology has developed rapidly. I recently returned from a speaking tour in Manila, Bangkok, and Singapore. To my dismay, at least a third of my audience participants had cellular telephones with them. What's worse—they answered incoming calls while still seated in the front row and tried to carry on a conversation during the middle of a workshop project with their peers.

The telephone, no doubt, is a productivity tool. But it has the potential to destroy your tranquillity and even create danger. How many car accidents or near accidents have you seen caused by someone heavily involved in a phone conversation from their car? And that's to say nothing of the expense for each person who decides to call you on your mobile for nothing more important than to ask you about the weather in your lane.

The call-waiting feature is another temptation for a tirade from the first caller you've left on hold while you investigate the second beeping in your ear and decide which caller is most important.

And because the telephone is ubiquitous, we treat telephone conversations casually, talking far longer than we need or want to. Productivity experts have verified the tremendous savings of electronic message systems simply because the "chit-chat" time is reduced when we leave messages rather than speak in real time. Those tempted to call for a chat might be shocked at how many minutes they actually fritter away. If you think time may be slipping away from you on the telephone, make a habit of checking your watch when you start and end a call. Or, get the statistics from your computer software package as it logs calls. Is this how you want to invest your time?

Finally, do you really want to be that closely "in touch"? Do you really want someone to be able to reach you every moment of your waking hours? I can tell you from the battered looks on the faces of sales and service reps that I encounter, the answer is a definite no. Why do you think some companies offer pager pay for someone to keep a beeper at their bedside? It's one thing for this constant contact to be mandated by an employer, but quite another for people to put themselves in this position of their own free will.

Ask yourself if the phone is a tool or a trifler for you?

TIME FOR A CHECKUP

Have you ever had an accident, or near-accident, using a car phone?

Do you really want to be "on call" 24 hours a day?

Do you often have to apologize to an angry caller for keeping him or her on hold while you answer another incoming call?

Do you often answer the phone with an exasperated tone of voice simply because you are tired of hearing it ring?

PROTECT YOURSELF FROM NUISANCE CALLERS AND VISITORS

Guard your own spare moments. They are like uncut diamonds.—RALPH WALDO EMERSON

"I'm going to go home (or to the conference room/lounge/hotel room) to get some work done," is a statement I'm hearing increasingly often from friends and clients. The implication is that their office has become Grand Central Station, not a place to get serious work done. Why should these people have to go somewhere besides their office to work?

The open-door policy proved a great gesture thirty years ago. It helped flatten the management hierarchy by letting employees know they were welcome to touch the brass, to speak up with new ideas and suggestions for better ways of doing things.

The open culture still has promise and purpose, but carried to the extreme, the policy has robbed many people of their productive work time. If this has happened in your environment and you can't find four hours of uninterrupted work time to complete a project, then you need to modify your habits.

If you don't have a personal assistant to screen calls and take messages, trade off the chore with a peer. You take messages for her or him during certain periods and vice versa. Or, put your phone on the message service and close your door; then retrieve your voice mail every two or three hours. Or, do not respond to knocks. Or, hang out a sign asking not to be interrupted before X time except for emergencies. Or, establish a "quiet hour" when no one makes internal calls or visits.

As soon as you start making exceptions and breaking your own rules, so will everyone else. Whatever system you use, enforce it and abide by it yourself.

TIME FOR A CHECKUP

Can you work in your own office uninterrupted for a four-hour stretch?

Do you have to arrive at the office early or stay late to get your important projects completed in solitude?

GET OUT OF
E-MAIL AND
VOICE-MAIL JAIL

We do more talking progress than we do progressing.
—WILL ROGERS

We've come full-circle. From saving letter-writing time by sending an informal electronic or voice message to saving time and frustration by putting the message in a letter. Puzzled by that seemingly contradictory pronouncement?

Granted, on many occasions, sending a quick E-mail or leaving a voice mail is the fastest and easiest way to communicate.

But not so on *all* occasions with *all* organizations and people. This past year I got caught in voice-mail jail with a New York publisher in the midst of a merger. I called the last editor of record to ask that rights be returned on a particular book. When several days passed with no response, I phoned again and got another voice message stating that the editor would be out for two weeks and giving the number of another person to call in her absence. I called the second person—only to get a voice recording to call a third person. The loop continued through fourteen people, with the last voice recording telling me to call the original person at the original number. Through all these messages and callbacks, it took me five months to complete the loop—with no resolution at all.

I finally wrote a letter—a physical message that went to a real person, who got me a real answer within two weeks.

Technology has its moments of glory. But don't let it exasperate you and waste your time when things—or people—malfunction.

TIME FOR A CHECKUP

Do you ever feel like screaming or cursing when caught in an E-mail or voice-mail trap set by some unsuspecting soul?

Are you infuriating other people by leaving incomplete, vague, or outdated electronic answering messages for your unsuspecting callers?

Is your whole E-mail and voice-mail system a hoax to stall for time?

DON'T MEET WITHOUT A REASON— A GOOD ONE

Sometimes I get the feeling that the two biggest problems in America today are making ends meet—and making meetings end.—ROBERT ORBEN

Unless your job is defined as meeting facilitator, find more productive ways to accomplish your goals. Will any of these substitutes do the trick? A letter or memo giving the same information? A written request for suggestions and other input? A teleconference? An electronic meeting?

If you must have a live meeting in real time, consider these suggestions for making your meetings productive and short:

- Have a stand-up meeting in the hallway or in someone's office.

- Schedule meetings for the last thirty minutes of the day so everyone is conscious of time.

- Schedule meetings for odd times (9:20) so people know you're serious about the start time.

- State the ending time so people know that you don't intend to let the discussion go on for hours, reeling out of control and toward no conclusion or action.

- Prepare an agenda and send it out ahead of time so people come with ideas and relevant information at hand.

- State any pertinent information people should bring with them.

- Cancel or postpone the meeting if key people cannot be present.

- Have a competent meeting leader or facilitator to keep the meeting moving.

- Bring another project with you to work on in case the meeting starts late.

Meet in real time only for a really good reason.

Time for a Checkup

Do you understand your role as a meeting leader?

Do you understand meeting processes as a meeting participant?

Do you require people to come to meetings just because they're regularly scheduled?

Do you always prepare an agenda and stick to it?

Do you start and end on time?

RECYCLE YOUR ACCOMPLISHMENTS

*A "sensational new idea" is sometimes just an old idea with its
sleeves rolled up.*—ANONYMOUS

Whatever you save is, later, like something found.—YIDDISH SAYING

In 1986 I did massive research on excess paperwork in
corporations and wrote a book called *Cutting
Paperwork in the Corporate Culture* aimed at senior
executives. Six years later, I recycled those ideas into
Clean Up Your Act, a book of personal tips aimed at
helping individuals get the paperwork off their desk. It
took me only twenty-eight hours to write that book. In
1996, it took about ten minutes to recycle a few of
those tips into a chapter of this book. How so fast?
Recycled ideas with a new slant.

It doesn't matter the process or purpose. We also
recycled my daughter's wedding invitations list into a
list for my parents' golden wedding anniversary and
finally into our change-of-address list for friends and
family.

The last time I planned a surprise birthday party for
a family member, we kept our things-to-do list with
information about where we purchased the special decorations, what games we played, and the menu items
that brought so many compliments. For the next party,
the plans will be much quicker.

Several years ago, I conducted a series of public workshops around the country on how to write and sell book manuscripts to major publishing houses. We kept good records of what groups of people would have particular interest because of their chosen career, appropriate mailing lists, good places to advertise, and our response rates from each effort. This year when we decided to conduct another such public seminar, half the work was done.

Keep this-is-how-we-did-it records so each time becomes easier and quicker to repeat the process. Projects should get easier—not harder—as you repeat them.

TIME FOR A CHECKUP

Do you frequently have to reinvent the wheel for recurring projects?

Do you remember whom you called the last time you needed a negative made from a print?

Do you have at your fingertips a list of people or companies you can call for odd jobs or projects (photographers, printers, cleaning/carpet service, lawn service, pianist, videographer, soloist, computer consultant)?

CREATE SYSTEMS AND ROUTINES FOR THE DAILY DUTIES

Have a time and place for everything, and do everything in its time and place, and you will not only accomplish more, but have far more leisure than those who are always hurrying, as if vainly attempting to overtake time that had been lost.—TYRON EDWARDS

Good order is the foundation of all things.—EDMUND BURKE

Routine is calming; random is chaotic. Systems and routines make things faster, cheaper, better. In our office, we've mapped our processes for preparing books, speeches, and training courses, right along with our routine office procedures for handling mail, shipping products, and invoicing.

Hotels teach their housekeeping crews how to clean a guest room in eight minutes. How? By having the appropriate tools at hand and by moving in a prescribed order around the room, doing things in the same way in the same sequence each time. Practice makes a perfect, quick routine.

It works at the office: If you collect the same information over and over, can you compile a form to hand to your customer or employee? If you give out the same the same questions, can you prepare a flyer available to visitors and callers? If you give the instructions for operating the same equipment, can you post the procedure near the equipment? If you respond to customers about the same products, can you create boilerplate letters and proposals ready for customizing? If you have a typical weekly staff meeting, can you use the same boilerplate agenda for customizing?

Systems work at home as well as in the office: Do you eat first or dress first? Do you plug in the coffee before or after you shower? Do you wake the kids before or after you start breakfast? Do you buy birthday greeting cards at the grocery story or the gift shop? Do you drop off the cleaning before or after work? Do you serve company buffet meals from the kitchen counter, the center island, or the range top? Do you wash white clothes on Monday evening or Saturday morning?

Systemize to minimize the thought process and wasted energy for routine tasks and schedules.

Tɪᴍᴇ ғᴏʀ ᴀ Cʜᴇᴄᴋᴜᴘ

Do you have current written processes to train new employees?

Do you have a desk manual for your routine tasks?

Do you have a routine schedule to get the family out the door each morning with minimal surprises?

Do you have a routine cleaning, laundry, and shopping schedule at home, and does all the family know what it is?

PRACTICE PROJECT MANAGEMENT IN YOUR PERSONAL LIFE

The Ninety-Nine Rule of Project Schedules: The first ninety percent of the task takes ninety percent of the time, and the last ten percent takes the other ninety percent.—ARTHUR BLOCK, MURPHY'S LAW

What works well in business often fails to get translated to personal life. Like projects. Instead of letting big chores or projects overwhelm you, handle the household tasks like work "projects." Sending Christmas cards. Decorating for the holidays. Cleaning the house for weekend company. Getting ready to leave on vacation. Shopping for school clothes. Moving. Doing tax returns. Creating a filing system for the household. Landscaping the backyard.

In a nutshell:

- Set the goal. (To clean and organize the garage.)
- Set the deadline. (Is this an hour's project? A weekend project? A summer project?)
- Divide the project into subtasks. (Buy shelving. Buy household cleaners to scrub stuff. Buy a hose and

ladder. Paint the storage cabinets. Collect the old toys stored there to give to Goodwill. Repair the concrete crack. And so forth.)

- Decide on the best sequence for the subtasks. (You don't want to pull everything off the shelves and then discover you have no sandpaper to prepare the wood for paint.)
- Gather your resources. (Information, tools, equipment.)
- Make work assignments. (Who is best suited for which subtasks? Will their schedules accommodate the work to be done?)
- Monitor your progress. (Who's not doing their job and why? Do you have all the resources you need?)
- Celebrate the completion of the project.

TIME FOR A CHECKUP

How many times a week do you have to go to the store unexpectedly for something you or another family member forgot the last trip?

Do you frequently run out of household staples?

Do you have to iron or wash clothes so somebody can wear them within the hour?

How smoothly do the major household projects run—like vacations or moves or tax preparation?

CONSOLIDATE SIMILAR ACTIVITIES

Plan ahead. It wasn't raining when Noah built the ark.
—RICHARD CUSHING

Take a lesson from the mosquito. She never waits for an opening—she makes one.—KIRK KIRKPATRICK

Retailers report that customers come into their stores asking for things that allow them to do two things at the same time—like an exercise bike that has a reading rack to hold a book, like a walkman with an audio player to listen to self-improvement tapes, like a television with insets for the second picture, like telephones with long cords to walk around the kitchen while cooking, like cars that have phones and portable TVs, like grocery stores that sell stamps. We even prefer one-handed food like chicken nuggets, corndogs, and ice cream on a stick so we can eat while doing something else.

But you'll waste time, energy, and brainpower when changing activities randomly. Avoid the stop-and-start pattern of dissimilar activities: Make a call. Run across town to make a purchase. Write a letter. Calculate figures for a report. Then make another call.

Instead, bunch your calls. Then run errands on the other floors in the building. Then write the three letters, memos, or reports you need to get out.

But do notice the suggestions in this book for *not* doing so many things at once so you can enjoy and concentrate on what you're doing. The determining factor is efficiency. For pleasure, do one thing at a time. For efficiency, do similar activities simultaneously.

TIME FOR A CHECKUP

Do you find yourself changing clothes several times a day because you're not dressed appropriately for various tasks at hand—you're wearing jeans for errands and then having to put on a suit for a client appointment?

Do you frequently interrupt yourself and break your concentration by stopping a task to run a quick errand or take a call?

At the end of the hour or day, do you have ten projects in progress and none completed?

OPTIMIZE YOUR SCHEDULING

BUILD WHITE SPACE INTO YOUR CALENDAR

The real secret of how to use time is to pack it as you would a portmanteau, filling up small spaces with small things.
—HENRY HADDOW

You have wasted time if a specific project gets delayed (waiting on approvals, preferences, or key information) and you've planned too little for the day or week. However, if you schedule too much, you feel frustrated that you're never finished at the end of the day or week. Your morale drops.

To schedule your work most effectively, build white space into your calendar. Do not schedule enough tasks to consume every working and waking moment. Then if interruptions come, you won't experience the domino effect and have to play catch-up.

In my typical scheduling, I plan to about 80 percent capacity when I'm going to be in the office and about 50 percent capacity just after returning from a trip.

That means for a 50-hour workweek, I schedule onto my calendar about 40 hours of work, knowing that another 10 hours of "stuff" will appear unexpectedly.

If I'm surprised by having no unplanned projects land on my desk, then I can flip the calendar and get a jump on next week—a real morale booster—or simply knock off early.

TIME FOR A CHECKUP

Do you feel as though you're always playing catch-up by noon of each day?

Do you end each week disheartened that you didn't get finished with all you had planned to do?

GET A FAST START

If it were done when it is done then it were well it were done quickly.—ANONYMOUS

No one ever climbed a hill just by looking at it.—ANONYMOUS

No one can build a reputation on what he's going to do tomorrow.—ANONYMOUS

If you've ever played on a sports team, you know the difference in the players' morale when they're leading all the game or playing catch-up from the start.

Work creates a similar feeling. Do you typically plan projects by putting the deadline on your calendar and then working backward with interim dates? If so, reverse the process. Put an immediate start date on the calendar and see how much freedom and flexibility you feel about the deadline.

When you delay projects—or even schedule a begin date that *should* allow adequate time for the work—you chance running into the unexpected. Then you must complete the project with a mental weight around your mind.

To lift your morale and work like a winner, get a fast start on big projects. Assume the project will take much longer than you hope. If it goes as planned with no surprises and you finish early, you'll be delighted and relieved.

TIME FOR A CHECKUP

Do deadlines give you headaches?

Do you do less than your best on important projects simply because you're pushing a deadline and don't have time to double back and do things differently?

AVOID WORK-AND-WAIT PATTERNS

He that hopes hereafter to look back with satisfaction upon past years, must learn to know the present value of single minutes.
—SAMUEL JOHNSON

Waiting for approvals/opinions, information, equipment, or resources is a major timewaster, creating havoc with scheduling. But inevitably you'll have to wait. Even CEOs have to wait on decisions by the board of directors, responses from the public about new products or services, or return phone calls from the press.

So, adapting to the pattern is your choice by default. Here are some tactics than can minimize, if not prevent, such slowdowns:

- Get other people's buy-in on the due dates before you schedule tasks.
- Call people and explain your priorities and urgency.
- Offer to help people do the work or collect the information you need.
- Let people know you don't have to have the information in formal or final form.

- Let people know you'll take incomplete information until the total information is available.
- Ask people whom they can refer you to for further help or information.
- Escalate the problem to your own supervisor to negotiate the information at a higher level.
- Remind everyone involved that you need the information as soon as it's available.

When nothing else can be done and you're still stalled, move to your next project and stop spinning your wheels.

TIME FOR A CHECKUP

Do you wait on the same people repeatedly?

Do you routinely use "I'm waiting" situations as excuses for not meeting deadlines?

Do others know you're waiting for information/action from them?

CONCENTRATE

Don't Invite Interruptions

What you perceive, you should filter, so you can focus on those things which are useful and applicable to your own dictionary of the world.—Richard Saul Wurman

I didn't realize how focused I could be until one day when I heard my 6-year-old coming down the hallway with his friend. I had just finished a novel chapter and turned off my computer a little early for the day. Feeling really good about finishing, I was sitting at my desk, staring out my window on the beautiful summer afternoon. Son Jeff and friend David tiptoed in behind me. Jeff said aloud behind my back, "Watch this, David. I'm going to talk to her and she won't even hear me. Mom, . . . Mom, . . . earth to Mom?"

I swirled around to surprise him, "Yes, Jeff?"

He was startled—and irritated that I'd heard him on first call. I'd completely ruined his demonstration of my concentration. But he made his point. I do concentrate on the task at hand.

Do you invite interruptions that break your concentration? Even an amused facial expression will lure people to your desk to strike up a conversation. Do you have "toys" and gadgets on your desk that people feel compelled to touch as they pass? Do you keep several projects within sight on your desk so that you're tempted to go from one to the other randomly? Do you stop to take calls while you're trying to do creative work? Do you ask other people for opinions and then think about your rebuttal rather than listen to their response? Contrary to what many people claim, you cannot do two things at once as well as you could by concentrating on one task at a time until it's complete.

Generally it takes longer to do three tasks with divided attention than to do them one at a time with full attention.

Time for a Checkup

Do you have your office and work space arranged to minimize distractions from the outside?

Do you turn off background music or TV when trying to work?

Do you keep your door closed to signal others that you don't want interruptions?

MAKE AS FEW UNIMPORTANT DECISIONS AS POSSIBLE

Time has a wonderful way of weeding out the trivial.
—RICHARD BEN SPIR

A few weeks ago I walked into a stationery shop to place an order for fifty invitations to a wedding rehearsal dinner. As I began to thumb through the sample books to make a selection of cards and verses, the clerk accosted me with questions: Do you want a flat invitation or one that folds over? Do you want something formal or informal? Do you want a border or no border? Do you want white, ecru, or a pastel? Do you want a standard verse, or will you compose your own?

After we made the card, color, and verse selection, she started to write up the order and I thought I was home free, still within my fifteen-minute time frame. Then there was a deluge of more questions: Black ink or color? Style of printing? Vertical or horizontal layout? Lined or unlined envelope? Return address printed on the front left corner of the envelope, on the back flap, or not at all? RSVP to be open or request "regrets only"? Should the RSVP contain phone number, address, and name—or only the number, or only the address? Should the address block be centered at the bottom or flush left or flush right? Time, date, and year to be spelled out or printed numerically? The room to come before the name of the hotel or after? Print *p.m.* or *o'clock* after the time?

After I rattled off the answers to her, the clerk wanted to read my choices back to me to make sure she had recorded them correctly. What I expected to be a fifteen-minute selection took nearly forty-five minutes.

Alvin Toffler said it first in his 1970 book *Future Shock:* "We are . . . racing toward 'overchoice.'" Make as few unimportant decisions as possible. Do you really need to spend two minutes at the grocery story selecting pink or plain toothpicks?

Time for a Checkup

How many times do you read through the menu before ordering lunch?

How many times do you change clothes before going to work each morning?

How long do you spend reading labels before purchasing a sack of nails at the hardware store?

How many pairs of hosiery do you routinely buy at one time?

Do you care what color your bank checks are?

MAKE FASTER DECISIONS WHEN THE DECISIONS ARE NOT IRREVOCABLE

You can never get much of anything done unless you go ahead and do it before you are ready.—ANONYMOUS

Indecision is the graveyard of intentions.—ANONYMOUS

Procrastination is the fertilizer that makes difficulties grow.
—ANONYMOUS

Speaking to an audience in Dallas, General Norman Schwarzkopf shared his philosophies of decision making and leadership. He told about taking over a new job early in his career. Sitting in one of the first meetings, his officers presented him with a problem and several courses of action. They pointed out to him that his predecessor had been postponing a decision for the previous five years to allow time to "study" the problem. After listening to his newly acquired staff outline the pros and cons of the salient issues, he made a decision and ended the meeting.

One of the men stayed behind afterward to ask him where he'd learned such superior decision making skills—understanding the problem and its ramifications and coming to the right decision in such a brief time.

Schwarzkopf summarized his philosophy this way: If it wasn't the right decision, he had confidence in the rest of his staff to make it the right decision. He went on to explain his reasoning about decision making. If somebody had been studying the decision for five years, then chances were that no new information was going to surface and that there were no clear-cut answers. Some decision needed to be made so they could take action—any action. Even if the decision were the wrong one, that would probably become apparent soon enough, in which case the staff would go to work to do what was necessary to make it the right decision under the circumstances.

Sounds pretty logical to me.

Why do we drag our feet with decisions? We're afraid of making the wrong decision and reaping the consequences. We don't have a system or steps for making sound decisions at all. We're trying to gather too much information to remove the risk factor. We're afraid of making a reasoning error in a hurry and under stress. All those reasons are good ones. But they certainly slow us down and create mental anguish that can paralyze us.

Assess the relevant facts about a situation. Gather information that's available. Develop alternatives. Identify and evaluate negative consequences. Decide. Take action.

In the process of building a new house, we were driving through subdivisions of custom homes. I commented to the realtor, "It surprises me to see so many builders in here building 'spec' homes with such a high price tag. You'd think that if somebody were going to pay these prices for a house, they'd at least want to have a say in designing it."

The realtor responded, "It's the time factor. People who can afford these homes have such a busy life that they don't have the time to make all the related decisions. It's easier for them to let the builder finish it and then go back and modify it as necessary."

Few decisions in life are completely irrevocable.

Time for a Checkup

How long does it take you to buy the typical Christmas or birthday present?

Has "I'm waiting on more information" become a tactic for delay in making risky decisions?

Which decisions in your organization have never been reversed?

DELEGATE PROBLEMS AND DECISIONS TO YOUR SUBCONSCIOUS

One of the unfortunate things about our education system is that we do not teach students how to avail themselves of their subconscious capabilities. —BILL LEAR

Have you ever experienced the situation in which you were trying desperately to remember something—say the title of a movie or song, someone's name, or the answer to a riddle? You give up trying to remember, put the incident behind you, and go on about your business. Then two days later, the movie or song title, riddle answer, or name just pops into your mind! That's an example of your subconscious working on the assignment for you.

Make more conscious use of that feature of your brain. When you have a problem or issue that has you puzzled or paralyzed with indecision or inaction, consciously put it out of your mind and promise yourself to let your subconscious work on it while you go on about your conscious business. Presto. In a few hours, days, or weeks, the "answer" or "alternative" or a clear course of action may come to you "out of the blue." Since a writer friend made me aware of how the subconscious works, it has become one of my most productive writing techniques, diminishing my stress over such frustrating blanks in creative problem solving.

When faced with a difficult decision or situation in which you can't even create alternatives or options, often your subconscious can do a better job than your conscious mind.

TIME FOR A CHECKUP

Have you ever had "ah-ha" answers pop out of your mind hours after you gave up on remembering something? (Then consciously delegate projects to the subconscious.)

Are you confusing delegation to your subconscious with procrastination? (They're not the same.)

LEARN IN LAYERS RATHER THAN IN GULPS

Everybody gets so much information all day long that they lose their common sense.—GERTRUDE STEIN

People learn what you teach them, not what you intend to teach them.—ANONYMOUS

It is only when we forget all our learning that we begin to know.—HENRY DAVID THOREAU

Sitting in a seminar all day or learning a new skill or information on the job can be mentally exhausting. Instead of a crash course, relax and learn information for the long-term—in layers rather than in gulps.

First, get an overview of the information or skill you need to learn. Then try to pinpoint the main ideas and recall them to yourself on several occasions. Next, focus on the details and your use for those details. (As you learn, ask: "Why will I need to know this? How can I use this information?") Finally, understand what something is not. (Is this not true when X? Is this procedure not to be followed in cases like Y?)

The layered learning concept makes learning massive amounts of information a manageable task. Instructors who must learn lecture materials to present to communication classes master up to thirty-two hours of information by learning layers at a time. They observe the classes to get familiar with what has to be learned. Then they divide the information in chunks and learn the three to eight key points in each section. Next, they master the detail surrounding each concept. Then they learn how to apply the principles to various audience needs and uses. Finally, they learn what the information does *not* mean by focusing on answers to frequently asked questions. That's layered learning for long-term use.

And it's much less fatiguing—and much more thorough and rewarding—than the cram courses we encountered in college.

TIME FOR A CHECKUP

Do you read the entire instructions (including any precautions and safety matters) before beginning a task?

Do you preview an article or book before starting to read the first chapter?

Do you learn a new software package by focusing on the few features you will use most frequently?

Do you routinely ask the "whys" when you learn the "hows" of a process?

RECOGNIZE WHEN YOU'RE "PIDDLING" TO PROCRASTINATE

If you want to make an easy job seem mighty hard, just keep putting off doing it.—OLIN MILLER

One of these days is none of these days.—ENGLISH PROVERB

Procrastination is a habit common to most of us at one time or another. We procrastinate when a job seems overwhelming, unpleasant, boring, risky, or unclear. Sometimes procrastination serves as a technique to get others' sympathy or help or to irritate them or sabotage their goals.

"Piddling" on purpose is fine. That can be restful. But piddling when you think you're busy is self-delusion. For some of us, myself included, piddling is usually a sign of delayed decision making or procrastination. Decide which.

If the piddling is procrastination, "tease" yourself with small, doable chunks. Forget perfection and creativity; just start somewhere. Mark your place and the next action to be done before you stop work. Stop and start when things are going well—not when you're stuck. (Otherwise, you'll never want to go back to the project.) If you're stuck on a project, give your subconscious time to work out a solution. Reward any progress at all. Start with the most dreaded part so you can get it over with. Then being over that biggest hump, you'll gain energy for the rest.

If the piddling is delayed decision making, bring the decision to the forefront of your mind and focus on it until you decide. After the decision, you'll be surprised how much more you can get done in the same hours.

TIME FOR A CHECKUP

Do you spend a disproportionate amount of time at the start of a project and then seem to move through the rest of the project much more quickly?

Do you view a typical project as a monumental task, or do you consider it a series of small steps in a longer process?

Do you find yourself doing unnecessary or easy chores in prime work time?

Do you prefer to "sleep on it" before starting a project "the right way"?

Do you prefer that your supervisor, a committee, or team members concur before you make "tough decisions"?

Do you frequently postpone tackling tough projects because you feel "too tired"?

PIDDLE ON PURPOSE

Half our life is spent trying to find something to do with the time we have rushed through life trying to save.
—WILL ROGERS

Make your piddling purposeful—to relax. Tell yourself that it's okay not to spend every waking moment on a productive task. Allow yourself some time to piddle as a refreshing break.

Walk through the office and see who you can find to chat with. Check out the vending machines for new surprises lurking there. Walk through the lobby and notice the visitors sitting there. Gaze out the windows and watch the passersby.

At home, walk through the house and really look around to see what's there. Play with your knickknacks and souvenirs on the shelves and in the cabinets. Thumb through magazines or surf the Internet.

Purposefully let your mind wander and disengage without guilt. Tell yourself that you've chosen to piddle for a break, and do it without guilt or hurry.

TIME FOR A CHECKUP

Do you feel guilty when you leaf through a magazine aimlessly?

Do you feel "caught" when someone walks into your office or your house and finds you not engaged in a productive task?

Do you ever just let your mind float free in the middle of the workday?

DON'T CONFUSE ACTIVITY WITH RESULTS AND MEANING

It's not enough to be industrious—so are the ants. What are you industrious about?—HENRY DAVID THOREAU

Some people seemed to be wired for hyperactivity. They can't sit still at home or at work. They're calling, visiting, coordinating, negotiating, donating, organizing, pleading, complaining, writing, buying, storing, learning, washing, polishing, arguing, walking, cycling, eating, cooking, doctoring, planting, planning, selling, filing, insuring, driving, attending, consolidating, dividing, or otherwise staying busy. If given a chance, they'll tell you what they have yet to go on their to-do list.

But accomplishment is another matter. In all your hustle and bustle, are you achieving results for your family, your organization, even yourself? Is the activity important to you? Does it make your life meaningful?

Time for a Checkup

Do you feel constantly fatigued?

Do you participate in some activities just because you always have?

Do people frequently tell you that you need to "slow down"?

Do people frequently comment on your excessive or abundant "energy"?

Do people frequently ask, "Do you ever rest?"

Are you overly busy to avoid dealing with something else that's missing in your life?

DRAIN THE BOTTLENECKS IN YOUR LIFE

No farmer ever plowed a field by turning it over in his mind.
—A<small>NONYMOUS</small>

In the orchard of opportunity, it is better to pick the fruit than to wait for it to fall.—A<small>NONYMOUS</small>

Have you ever observed how bottlenecks work to back up action and bring things to a standstill? Bottlenecks in traffic when one lane is under construction. Bottlenecks in getting a massive amount of food through your sink disposal. Bottlenecks at work when a manager won't make a decision. Bottlenecks of paperwork when one department lags behind others in processing.

Many people's lives contain bottlenecks that slow them down and keep them from experiencing balance in their emotions and in their physical activity. They long to take up new hobbies or enjoy new entertainment, but then there's no money to pay for it. They want to quit working such long hours, but then there are high expenses and bills coming due every month. They long to spend time with a spouse who has different life goals and "can't find the time." They get excited about starting new projects and leisure activities, but their lack of self-discipline keeps them from ever mastering a new skill.

Whatever the bottleneck—no money, high living expenses, spouse, self-discipline, long hours at work—it will keep recurring to sabotage your goals until you do something about it. Pinpoint that recurring "thing" that keeps you from doing what you want to do, deciding what you want to decide, or carrying through with what you start.

TIME FOR A CHECKUP

Do you start a lot of projects and finish only a few?

Do you keep dealing with the same emotional issues over and over?

Do family members and friends tell you in so many words to "put your money where your mouth is?"

Do you hear yourself giving the same excuses over and over for why you're not getting to do what you want to do?

WORK ACCORDING TO YOUR NATURAL RHYTHM

HIDE THE CLOCK

I must govern the clock—not be governed by it.—GOLDA MEIR

Do you eat when the clock says it's noon? Have you ever worked through lunch and not missed it? Do it more often. Hide the clock at work or at home at night.

I've discovered that I can get about twice as much done each day when I'm writing a book or developing a course or speech if I do it at home when I'm not conscious of the daily schedules of others. I can get up at six and go straight to the computer. Then about 10 o'clock when I'm ready for a break, I have breakfast. If I feel the need to stretch my legs at 2:00 p.m., that's when I exercise.

Everything in the universe moves according to some rhythm. The tides. The plants. The sun and moon. The rule of supply and demand. The bond and interest rates. So does the human body and spirit.

Take advantage of that rhythm. Learn how your inner clock runs during the day, during particular seasons of the year, during peak emotional events and times. Take advantage of your peak periods for productivity. Focus and complete one thing at a time while in your peak mode.

Don't let the mechanical clock tell you what to do. If you break at the wrong time, you may never regain the momentum that would have seen you through a complete task in one setting.

TIME FOR A CHECKUP

How often do you skip meals if you're "on a roll" with a project?

How often do you stay late to finish a project, even when the clock says it's quitting time?

Have you ever been so involved in a self-improvement course that you complete three or four lessons at one sitting?

Have you ever worked past dark on an outdoors project just because you wanted to finish?

VARY THE RHYTHM OF YOUR ROUTINES

Routines can be good. They get us through the day with minimal thought and energy. But sometimes that sameness of routine saps life of meaning, spontaneity, learning, or excitement.

If you have a monotonous job and personal schedule, add variety by varying your days and hours. If you usually eat out on Friday nights, try eating out on Wednesday evenings. If you usually call on the field offices on Thursday, make your visits on Monday for a few weeks. If you typically take the freeway to work, try the back roads one day a week. If you deliver contracts between 9 a.m. and noon, deliver them the last stop of the day for a change.

Move staff meetings from Monday mornings to Friday afternoons. Park your car on the roof rather than the basement. Shop at a different grocery store or in a different mall. Change flavors on your soft drinks. Invite company for Saturday brunch rather than Sunday lunch. Meet clients for breakfast rather than lunch.

Variety—and the resulting occasional mix-up—will add spice to an otherwise monotonous job or schedule.

TIME FOR A CHECKUP

When's the last time you changed your hairstyle?

When is the last time you took a different route to work?

How often do you change the cartoons in your work area or the photos in your bedroom?

Do you use the same salutations and closings on all your letters and memos?

Do you drink the same kind of coffee or tea—out of the same cup—every day?

When is the last time you ate lunch later than 2:00?

When's the last time you bought a new exercise video?

Can your spouse or children predict your exit comment as you head for the door each morning?

COMPLETE
THINGS

It ain't over til it's over.—Yogi Berra

Incomplete tasks leave you feeling depressed and wasted. Have you ever saved leftover pizza, intending to warm it in the microwave the next day for lunch? It tastes pretty good warmed over. But have you noticed how your appetite fades when you open that refrigerator and see that slice in there four days later? Two weeks later?

The same is true with leftover projects. They get stale and uninviting. You can't throw them out, but neither do you feel eager to tackle them again.

Sarah was my neighbor in Boulder, Colorado. A very talented, creative friend. But her house showcased unfinished projects. Take an imaginary walk with me next door and let me tell you what I saw one spring afternoon. On the living room sofa lay pages of scripts and props for an upcoming community theater play. The script was waiting until she got another inspirational burst of ideas. On the dining table were bunny ears—she was in the middle of making her toddlers costumes for a school play. In the kitchen, homemade bread was rising out of the bowl and onto the cabinet. The hallway was partitioned off with a bamboo screen from which hung red negligees. She'd decided to sell lingerie with one of those home-show companies and was in the midst of sending out catalogs to her friends and associates.

And so what did Sarah plan to do that evening? She invited my husband and me over for a candlelight dinner to celebrate our anniversary! A kind gesture, but needless to say, she always looked harried, frantic, tired.

Verify the phenomenon yourself. Aren't the days you go home from work the most exhausted, the days when you feel as though you started a thousand projects and finished none?

Bonuses come upon the *completion* of projects. Signed contracts come at the *end* of negotiations. Points go on the scoreboard only when the runner crosses the goal line. "Attempts" only make the scoreboard in football games—and only then as record of pass failures.

One thing completed is worth ten things on hold. And you'll feel energized by the accomplishment.

Time for a Checkup

How many projects do you have "open" on your desk?

How many self-improvement tapes have you purchased but not listened to?

How many books have you purchased but not read?

Do you still have the makings of last year's Christmas gifts on the drawing board at home?

How many recipes have you clipped but never concocted?

WORK IN MARATHONS

If you want to make good use of your time, you've got to know what's most important and then give it all you've got.
—LEE IACOCCA

Marathons serve two purposes: To catch up or to get ahead.

When you feel as though you're slipping further and further behind, decide to do a work marathon to catch up. Arrive early. Work late. Send out for food. Don't allow interruptions. Don't rework anything. Work fast and don't look up between projects. Put in three or four days like that, and you'll feel caught up enough to face the world again—or at least your desk—without getting depressed.

On other occasions, you may have monumental tasks before you and want to get a jump start on them. I do writing marathons when I begin new books. The book project always seems too overwhelming to tackle in sprints—only a few hours a day or only a few days a week. To say nothing of how stretching it out over a long period of time would reduce my enthusiasm for the project.

So I schedule a marathon and make it a big deal. I either hole up somewhere in a hotel on the road between speaking engagements, or schedule time away from the office to stay home so I don't have to get dressed up or go out for food. Finding a period of time that you want to make go faster also helps. For example, I often schedule these work marathons when my husband will be out of town; my long work hours keep me from thinking about missing him so much. I'm at the computer by 6 o'clock in the morning and often work until midnight, with a 45-minute exercise break and two or three 10-minute breaks for meals. When I'm tempted to stop and "check something" or go to the library or call a friend or phone the office to check my messages, I refuse to indulge myself with that particular excuse or distraction.

After I reach the halfway mark in the project, things move downhill with less emotional effort and self-discipline. I began to work faster and faster and accomplish more and more. When the marathon comes to an end, I have a finished manuscript and am in an exhilarated mood.

I've also done moving marathons (I hate to live out of boxes for weeks), sewing marathons (for the garments I have in mind's eye and can't find in the stores), cooking marathons (might as well since you've got every pot in the kitchen dirty anyway and can freeze future meals and desserts), and Christmas marathons (this feels like a mental vacation of sorts or a home redecoration project without the sawdust).

Try it. The exhilaration from what you accomplish will more than reduce the fatigue from the actual work.

TIME FOR A CHECKUP

Do you lose interest and enthusiasm for projects that drag on for long periods? (Know your maximum attention span—is it a week or a month?)

Do you get depressed when you get really far behind in your work?

Do you have a major project that you've been putting off for weeks or months because you don't have time to finish it?

TRAVEL TIGHT

Travel is educational. It teaches you that enough luggage is too much.—ANONYMOUS

When I was at home, I was in a better place; but travelers must be content.—WILLIAM SHAKESPEARE

Travel has become a little—or a lot—of everyone's job nowadays: travel to train, to sell, to meet, to motivate. Some people look forward to travel as opportunity to add a little spice to the routine work, to break the monotony of family life, and to have a little personal time and freedom. Others dread travel, considering it a major interruption to their life and a major stressor on the job.

Travel can create both—excitement and stress. Excitement of visiting new places, mingling with new people, learning new customs—even if only as far away and exciting as Crum, Texas. But there's also the stress. Of the physical work of preparing, planning, packing, repacking, and unpacking. The loneliness. The missed home events. The fear for physical safety. The threat of missed connections and inappropriate accommodations.

The key to keeping your balance while on the road is attitude and trappings.

First, attitude. Anything that you make up your mind to hate will be an unpleasant experience. But there are things you can do to make the time away from home more enjoyable: Take with you pleasant projects that you never seem to have time for at home—a good book, self-improvement or music tapes, audio or CDs, stationery to write long letters to friends. Take whatever you need to make you feel "at home." Your favorite perfume. Your favorite food. Your favorite robe.

Then there are the trappings. Unless you *need* the extras mentioned above to make your peace mentally, then leave all but the necessities at home. Make out your "equipment" list so you can pack quickly each time. Or better yet, keep your bags packed with duplicates.

Because I'm on the road about 80 to 100 days a year, I keep my bags packed with an extra hairdryer, curling iron, robe/gown/slippers, aerobics clothes, umbrella, alarm clock, breakfast bars, and cosmetic bag. My packing for each trip is then reduced to adding lingerie, suits, shoes, and jewelry.

Never pack with the intention of taking all you *might* need. Instead, pack with the thought, what can I get along *without?* Could I buy it if I really needed it? My all-time packing record is trekking all over the Far East for three weeks with only one garment bag.

The packing and unpacking time can be reduced if you use those containers with slots for all your goodies, the ones that you just remove from your travel bag and hang up on the bathroom door or closet rod to make the insides readily available. Those will cut the unpacking time to almost zilch.

The key to keeping your balance while traveling is your attitude before, during, and after takeoff and landing. Make reentry at home worthwhile.

Time for a Checkup

*Does the thought of travel—to any place—
exasperate you?*

*Can you wear the same suit or dress two or three
days in a row without boring yourself?*

*Do you use travel as an excuse to shuffle off home
responsibilities onto your spouse or other family
members that you could continue to handle from
the road?*

*Do you have a few "generic" accessories that will
work with more than one outfit?*

*Are you creating resentment toward yourself by
making other family members jealous of your
opportunity to travel and bypass responsibilities at
home?*

ENJOY THE ISOLATION OF COMMUTING

Happiness is in the heart, not in the circumstances.
—ANONYMOUS

Contentment is a matter of hoping for the best and making the best of what we get.—ANONYMOUS

More and more people and corporations are deciding that the best of all worlds includes telecommuting. If that's not possible, live as close to your work as possible. And when "as close as possible" is still too far, find a way to make your necessary commuting time either meaningful or useful.

During my stint in Houston, I had commuting time up to two hours one way for several years. When I was in a productive mood, I used the time for listening to self-development tapes, to review information for upcoming exams while working on an advanced degree, to plan parties, to think about and solve problems, and to pray and meditate.

My husband used to drive an hour each way to his job. When he changed jobs and lived only five minutes from his office, he actually missed the "downtime" between home and office in which he shifted gears mentally to get ready for the evening's activities.

The real difference in whether such time is a harried experience or a pleasant one is attitude.

TIME FOR A CHECKUP

What projects are suitable to make commute time productive?

What pleasant mental activities could you enjoy while commuting?

SEPARATE HOME FROM OFFICE WHEN YOU WORK FROM HOME

I do much of my creative thinking while golfing. If people know you are working at home they think nothing of walking in for a cup of coffee. But they wouldn't dream of interrupting you on the golf course.—HARPER LEE *(author of* To Kill a Mockingbird)

The number of individuals who work at home some of the time has increased by 50 percent since 1989. The figure now stands at more than 47 million workers, according to research done by the publishers of *Success* and *Working at Home* magazines.

No doubt about it, keeping balance in life is more difficult for some at-home workers—even when they're self-employed and are their own bosses. (According to the New York research firm FIND?SVP, 18.4 million home workers are self-employed.) Both personal life and home life seem to run together. For some people, myself included, this "running together" presents no problem because my work is fun and my fun is often work.

But for others who work at home, their work simply takes over their entire life against their will. If you're one of those people who needs these two distinct parts of your life to remain separate because you consider that separation part of your "balance" mindset, then here are some basic guidelines I've found helpful in working from home at times during my career.

- Don't be "home" when you're home. If you intend to get work done, let your family, neighbors, and friends know that you're keeping office hours the same as if you worked miles away. That means, don't answer the home phone line, don't go to the door if you're not expecting someone, don't offer taxi or babysitting service to your friends during the hours you intend to work.

- Decide on what hours you will stop and start work. Then stick to them—except for unusual circumstances and projects. (Having flexible hours, of course, is the reason many people enjoy working from home. The idea is not to let work hours extend into the evening and weekend until you forget to enjoy free time.)

- Use your office or work area only for work projects— not Scouts meetings, not phone calls to the symphony, not political campaigns.

- Don't drag work projects into other parts of the house so that work is staring you in the face at the breakfast table and on the night stand as you go to sleep.

- Stop talking about business when you go into other parts of the house to mix and mingle with the family—unless they ask about your work, as the typical family might after a day at the office.

- Do not work weekends—just because "it's there."

If, as I do, you enjoy your work so much that it has become your play—by choice—then don't worry about this distinct separation. Your life will feel whole whether an outsider would label specific activities work or play.

Time for a Checkup

Do you treat your home office space like real office space—with only work projects there?

Do you have files in the kitchen and food at the computer?

Do you welcome distractions from family and neighbors as part of your penchant for procrastinating on unpleasant work?

Do you stop and start work "when you feel like it"?

CREATE A MENTAL OASIS FOR CREATIVE THINKING AND WORK

Time is a sandpile we run our fingers in.—CARL SANDBURG

Imagination is more important than knowledge.
—ALBERT EINSTEIN

You cannot write the Great American Movie, your annual "accomplishment" report, or a $10 million client proposal without thinking space. For your creative projects, find a nonroutine environment.

For those who can afford the cost and travel time, you can go to a cabin or resort in the mountains or rent a hotel room. But closer, less exotic places will do: your backyard patio, the conference room down the hall, a friend's office, the neighborhood park, or the library. The idea is to see different scenery so that routine tasks and paperwork can't nag at you from the corner of your eye. Gaze at different walls or skies, relax in a different chair, hear different voices, hold a different coffee cup, feel a different breeze.

Sitting or standing out of the box helps you to think out of the box.

TIME FOR A CHECKUP

What's the last truly creative piece of work or single idea you've had? Where did the idea come to you?

How often do you do work away from your usual desk?

Do you value creativity in your life?

Where is your ideal place to let your mind roam free? How often do you go there?

PLAN "THINK ABOUTS" FOR LONG-TERM ISSUES

To possess ideas is to gather flowers; to think is to weave them into garlands.—ANONYMOUS

Whatever failures I have known, whatever errors I have committed, whatever follies I have witnessed in private and public life have been the consequences of action without thought.
—BERNARD BARUCH

Time was invented by the Almighty God in order to give ideas a chance.—NICHOLAS M. BUTLER

Rather than grapple with long-term, recurring issues as you go about your daily life, devote the time to them that they deserve.

There are two kinds of people in the world, the "thinkers" and the "sleepers." The thinkers approach life with their eyes open. The sleepers miss life because their eyes are closed.

Thinkers overhear a loud conversation at the lunch table and they analyze personality types and inner motivations of those involved. Sleepers overhear a loud conversation at the lunch table and complain to the management.

Thinkers see someone shoplift a piece of candy and they ponder our judicial system. Sleepers see someone shoplift a piece of candy and shrug that it's none of their business.

Thinkers hear a manager give a dull presentation and they speculate about ways to improve their own communication skills. Sleepers hear a manager give a dull presentation and they become bored and impatient.

Thinkers are quick-witted, analytical, vibrant, interested, and interesting. Sleepers are slow, insensitive, tired, bored, and boring.

To regain your own perspective when things become hectic, set aside time to think. Think about your goals. Think about what your family means to you. Think about the fun times you've had with a significant person. Think about how we can improve race relations. Think of ways to improve a friend's self-esteem. Think about a charitable fund-raising project for your community. Think about how you could become a better marriage partner and build stronger intimacy in your marriage. Think about what would motivate a coworker on the job.

"Think-about times" can help restore sanity for stay-at-home parents who have limited contact with other adults during the day or for technical professionals who interact mostly with machines rather than people.

These mental exercises about important issues rejuvenate your spirit and your intellect.

TIME FOR A CHECKUP

When is the last time you thought seriously about important issues outside your personal concerns of day-to-day life?

Is it your nature to complain about things, or take action to improve them?

CREATE CRATERS FOR TRUE CRISIS CRUNCHES

We cannot do everything at once, but we can do something at once.—CALVIN COOLIDGE

You've heard people insist that they are "at wit's end." Don't let yourself travel to that point when true crises comes.

Franklin Roosevelt understood the phenomenon when he commented in his inaugural speech, "We have nothing to fear but fear itself." An attitude of panic leads to actions that reflect panic. And panic displaces sound reasoning and logical action.

Consider the different responses with this analogy: Your boat fills with water in the midst of a big storm. You can frantically try to splash the water out with your hands, or you can keep your wits about you and take off your boots to make a bucket.

When you're surprised with a crisis at home or work—like an ill family member who suddenly requires all your attention and time or an unreasonable demand by a key customer with a short deadline—cut yourself some mental room to think. Take in a deep breath and acknowledge the crisis. Then remind yourself that you've handled similar crises before and that you can handle them again. Admit the fact that you will need to accomplish the near impossible and that you could easily panic if you gave in to the impulse.

Instead of collapsing mentally, carve out emotional room to let the crisis overflow into your psyche. Don't fight it. Make room to deal with it emotionally.

TIME FOR A CHECKUP

Do other people seem to depend on you in times of crises?

Is your immediate reaction in crises to look for others to blame?

Do you accept crises and deal with them, or do you panic helplessly, make poor decisions, and take senseless actions?

Do you perform at your best or your worst during true crises?

CAPTURE CRISES CREATED BY UNCONCERN

Ulcers are something you get from mountain-climbing over molehills.—LOCAL GOVERNMENT NEWSLETTER

Productivity is the true competitive advantage.—PETER DRUCKER

Often people in the workplace joke about crises as daily routine. You see signs and hear comments like these: "I'm out of the office—fighting fires." "It's just one crisis after another—get in line." "Is this a major crisis or a minor crisis—do I have time to get another cup of coffee?"

Don't assume crises on the job are normal. All offices and people don't operate in that climate. In fact, proper planning eliminates many "routine crises" while increasing productivity.

Some people treat all problems—no matter how small or routine—as if they're major crises. They overreact emotionally. Then overreacting emotionally, they make dumb decisions and take wrong actions. Worse still, when there's a true unpreventable crisis, no one takes their cries for help seriously.

It's dangerous to let crisis mode become habit.

TIME FOR A CHECKUP

Do people look at you like "business as usual" when you mention a crisis situation?

How many "crises" have you had at work in the last week?

How many "crises" have you had at home in the last week?

What's the difference between a crisis and a problem in your line of work?

AVOID LETTING YOUR STAFF SABOTAGE YOU

Those who enjoy responsibility usually get it; those who merely like exercising authority usually lose it.—MALCOLM FORBES

If you are working off the in-box that is fed you, you are probably working on the priority of others.—DONALD RUMSFELD

Unless you have excellent delegation skills, you may find your staff delegating work to you, thus controlling your schedule. Consider these comments from staff and coworkers as tell-tale signs.

- "I need you to review this to see if it's okay before I go further."
- "When will you have time to think about X and give me an approval?"
- "I don't think I should handle this without your seeing it first."
- "This is something you need to handle yourself."
- "I'm in over my head on this one. Can we talk?"
- "I can't get to that project right now—I'll let you know when I'm ready to talk about it."

Clearly, such comments signal that the staff, not the

supervisor, is in charge. To turn the tables and take back control of your own schedule, practice these responses.

- "You have my confidence. Please go ahead with the project."
- "I need the project completed in final form and ready to send the client by November 30. If you run into problems, keep me informed and let me know how you plan to handle them."
- "I'll consider the X situation when it becomes a higher priority for me. Now, I'm focused on Y."
- "I need you to manage the project. Here's the goal. . . . Here's the result we're trying to achieve. . . . Here's how I'll measure your success or failure on the project. . . . The budget is X. If you run into snags, call on Y and Z as resources. I'd like for you to check back with me if A or B happens. Unless I hear from you otherwise, I'll assume everything is on target and as planned."

Take corrective action when you get the feeling that you are having to work your schedule and your projects around the time frames and tasks set for you by your own staff.

TIME FOR A CHECKUP

Do you get the urge to hide when you see staff members approaching you?

Do you give open-ended assignments (with no deadline) to your staff, and then see those projects drag on and on without completion?

Does your staff know when you do—and do not—want progress reports?

Does your staff present problems *or* recommendations *to you?*

DELEGATE AT WORK, HOME, AND PLAY

We accomplish all we do through delegation—either to time or to other people.—STEPHEN R. COVEY

The best executive is the one who has sense enough to pick good men to do what he wants done and the self-restraint to keep from meddling with them while they do it.
—THEODORE ROOSEVELT

To lighten your workload to what a reasonably productive person should be able to accomplish, do an audit on yourself: What would happen if you didn't do a specific task at all? Could part of the task be eliminated? Could part of the task be delegated? Could someone else do the task better, faster, easier?

There are ample, understandable reasons people don't delegate to their staff: They don't want to put off unpleasant tasks on others. They don't want to upset someone with a task he or she won't like. They fear losing control of the project. They think they can do it faster themselves. They think they can do it better themselves. The staff is incapable of handling the project. They fear the staff will make irrevocable mistakes. They want the reputation for being a hardworking boss. They want to feel indispensable. They don't like dealing with the complaints from the staff about the project. They don't know how to delegate. The staff member refuses to accept responsibility for the project outcome.

When any of the above reasons make you reluctant to delegate, these guidelines will help:

- Give the job to the person most capable of doing it.
- Train and develop your staff.
- Make sure you give all vital information as you delegate: the goal, the result (measure of success or failure), the procedure, the deadline, the resources (budget, people), the worry factors.
- Follow up.
- Allow them to make decisions and mistakes.
- Give credit when they do a good job.
- Give constructive feedback when they make mistakes.

There are also understandable reasons people don't delegate to their committee of volunteers on social, civic, or professional projects: They want to control the project. They don't want their input to be ignored. They feel they have no authority to make the peer perform and don't want to be blamed for mistakes or inaction. They think, "If others wanted to do the task, they would have volunteered themselves." They want others to think they are a nice/capable/hardworking/committed person. They believe they have more time than their peers to devote to the project. They are afraid a peer will say no or complain about being asked to help.

When these give you pause with your peers, consider the following guidelines:

- Determine if you'd rather have help or have control.
- Request help rather than demand it.
- Give all vital information.
- Give plenty of recognition and credit for a job well done.
- Learn not to hear a no as a personal affront.

Last, consider the homefront. Parents also have understandable reasons for not delegating household projects to their children. They think they have more available time than their children. They want to "protect" their children from hard work and hassles. They think it will take more time to see that the child does the work than to do the task themselves. They think the child will not do the task the "proper" way. They fear the child will make mistakes. They want to avoid complaints and confrontations with the child.

If these reasons ring a bell with you as a parent, you may want to keep these guidelines in mind:

- Teach your child to be self-sufficient.
- Accept the fact that hard work and responsibility are actually good for a child.
- Allow children to do tasks their own ways as long as they accomplish the result you want.
- Tell a child if you expect him or her to do things your way.
- Allow the child to make mistakes without overreacting.
- Set deadlines and standards for completion and take the time to enforce them. (You'll need less time on this step as your child learns you mean what you say.)

- Consider dealing with complaints as part of raising a child.
- Give credit for a job well done.

Identify what is keeping you from delegating projects to others in your life and deal with it. You may do things faster and better *one* time, but over the long haul the pay-off for delegating far exceeds the hassle.

TIME FOR A CHECKUP

Do you routinely work longer hours than your staff?

Do you spend time on projects assigned to your staff when there's no particular problem?

How often do employees interrupt you for information necessary to complete their assigned projects?

Rather than teach others, do you frequently say to yourself, "I might as well do it myself" or "You'd better let me have a look at that first"?

Do you feel resentful when you see your spouse or children sitting in front of television or playing games while you work night after night and weekend after weekend?

TAKE RISKS FOR STIMULATION

The meaning of man's work is the satisfaction of the instinct for adventure that God has implanted in his heart.—PAUL TOURNIER

Far better it is to dare mighty things, to win glorious triumphs, even though checkered by failure, than to take rank with those poor spirits who neither enjoy much nor suffer much, because they live in the gray twilight that knows not victory nor defeat.—THEODORE ROOSEVELT

While gamblers welcome risks, most of us do everything in our power to avoid them. We go to parties and talk only to the people we already know. When eating in a restaurant, we order the same food from the menu every visit. We buy furniture only from stores that have a return policy.

But a low threshold for risk taking results in boredom and imbalance—sameness. There are three types of people who take on a new project or job: Those who ask, "What can I accomplish here?" Those who ask, "What do I have to do?" And those who ask, "What'll happen if I get it wrong?"

If you want to feel more control over your life, you have to be willing to step out of the sameness and take some risks—if for no other reason than mental stimulation. Here are some guidelines for taking and avoiding risks:

Don't decide to take a risk out of fear, anger, guilt, or depression.

Don't take more than one risk for each endeavor.

Do ask questions until you understand the situation and risk involved.

Do consider the consequences of the risk.

Do act decisively.

Do correct problems and alter your course as necessary along the way.

Be decisive enough to "cut bait" when circumstances warrant.

Most reasoned risks are not irreversible. To take control of your life is to risk new habits, new actions, new behaviors, new decisions, new acquaintances, new work, new play.

Time for a Checkup

How often do you invite new people to your parties?

Do you invest in different mutual funds that have a good track record?

How often do you buy "custom" gifts for your friends and family?

Do you go to different vacation spots each year?

Have you turned down new jobs or promotions just to avoid having to begin again in earning a boss's or coworker's respect for your abilities?

DUMP THE
BOSS GUILT

An organization can give a man the title of manager, but only the man can make himself into one.—JOSEPH MASON

"Boss guilt" is the feeling that you must outwork everyone on staff. Most probably, you do outproduce everyone on staff or you wouldn't be boss. But often bosses denigrate the fact that they produce more valuable work and instead translate "outwork" to mean "work longer hours."

Again, bosses make unrealistic demands on themselves even when they consider longer hours. If Joe works late on Monday, Cary works late on Tuesday, and Cathy works late on Wednesday, Juan works late on Thursday, and Tseuko works late on Friday, and Sherman works over the weekend, does that mean the boss should work late every day and all weekend to keep it even? You can see the fallacy in this reasoning.

Just because your staff doesn't operate as efficiently as you and get as much done during the regular workday is no reason that you as boss must punish yourself by working longer and longer hours.

Make sure your staff knows you judge work by accomplishment and results, not by hours spent on a task. Your own productivity and results should be apparent to your staff; dump the guilt and go home.

Time for a Checkup

Do you frequently hesitate to leave the office while another staff member is still at work?

When a member of your staff mentions work done on Saturday or Sunday or another day off, do you feel guilty and keep quiet about your relaxing weekend?

How do you judge your own commitment to the job—by results or by hours?

DEVELOP A PASSION FOR YOUR WORK OR WORK YOUR PASSION

If you love your job, you'll never have to go to work a day in your life.—CONFUCIUS

Work is love made visible.—KAHLIL GIBRAN

The time which we have at our disposal every day is elastic; the passions that we feel expand it, those that we inspire contract it, and habit fills up what remains.—MARCEL PROUST

One reason for feeling drained of spirit is feeling trapped in a job we do not enjoy. In earlier times, people put up with a boring job because work meant a paycheck, a means to an end. Today, work is the end.

If you doubt that, consider the behavior of those who are terminally ill among us. Even though they know they may have only six months to live, you often see them going to work for as long as they are physically able. Why? Work has become a major part of their lives. Of all our lives.

For those of us who enjoy our job, work is fun. Work pays for everything else we enjoy in life. Work provides our social relationships. Work allows us opportunity to live out our personal values. Work gives us an opportunity to serve others. Work provides personal satisfaction. Work gives us a chance to grow personally and feel successful. Work provides status. And besides, what else can you afford to do?

You may be saying, "Hold on a minute. I don't feel any of those things about work." If that's the case, then consider changing your work.

Nothing will make you feel more out of balance than spending eight to fourteen hours of your allotted twenty-four-hour day doing something that you dislike in exchange for a mere paycheck. Do you have a hobby that you enjoy? Do you have a cause that you believe in passionately? Do you want to develop skills in a fascinating area of interest that you've never fully explored?

Set about finding a way to make it happen. Although you may not be financially able to quit your current job tomorrow, make it your mission to rechart your future course. What new training do you need? Where can you get it? What money do you need? Where can you get it? Who do you need to know? Who can you ask for advice? Where can you go to investigate your passion further? How long will it take to make the changeover? What's the first step?

I'm not necessarily talking about a complete career change—changing your life's work from practicing law to teaching art. But perhaps a minor shift is all it would take to move you off the hectic track of hassles onto a less demanding and more satisfying career.

For example, instead of a general practitioner in medicine, you may want to become an ear, nose, and throat specialist. Instead of a being a realtor, you may want to manage properties. Instead of selling insurance, you may want to conduct seminars teaching new employees of large companies the insurance industry. Instead of managing the corporate public affairs department, you may want to consult with top officials who regularly meet the press. Instead of school administration as high school principal, you may want to move into the classroom. Instead of practicing law privately, you may want to be legal counsel at a local university or hospital.

Such changes may mean shorter hours, more or less travel, more or less people contact, more personal growth opportunities, less responsibility and stress, greater personal satisfaction.

One caution before jumping off the deep end into your own business venture without constructing a safety net: Investigate before you leap. Going into business for yourself sounds like the ultimate dream, but entrepreneurs can educate you on the long hours and stress that being totally responsible for your own livelihood brings. If that still sounds like a viable option after a realistic look, jump.

Rather than feeling trapped until retirement, set about making your work your fun. If you can't be passionate about your work, find a way to make your passion your work.

TIME FOR A CHECKUP

Do you generally like going to work on Wednesday mornings?

Can you express yourself and your values in your current job?

What work would you do even if you weren't paid to do it?

What do you daydream about doing?

What service would you like to render for others who are experiencing pain, despair, fear, growth, success, joy?

Figure the amount of money that you need to cover the absolute necessities—how important is the amount of your paycheck that exceeds that figure?

FIND FUN IN A MONOTONOUS JOB

No profit grows where is no pleasure taken.—William Shakespeare

Boredom is as positive a sensation as a toothache.—Lee S. Gunter

Everyone is a bore to someone. That is unimportant. The thing is to avoid being a bore to oneself.—Gerald Brenan

Fun and lighthearted behavior lift your spirit on the job. How to create fun when you have to be productive also? Don't equate fun with time-consuming activities; they aren't necessarily synonymous.

Two friends of mine used to bring cartoons to work to fax each other for a laugh a day. Hallway conversations over the latest shenanigans of customer X can produce a smile. Sharing the details of good news or successes in a coworker's personal life or career generates lighthearted relief.

Are you witty? Then pop off when others around you seem stressed.

Do you have a funny way of looking at the routine? Then share your views more often.

Can you create a commotion out of "a funny thing happened on the way to work"? Then do it.

Can you change locations for your work? Take it outside? Take it to the lounge? Do it standing rather than sitting? Sitting rather than standing? With your eyes closed? Wearing a Halloween mask?

Can you dress up? Can you dress down? Dress in costume to reflect your mood of the day?

Take a joke book to work and read a joke or anecdote once or twice a day. If it's really good, call someone and share it.

Can you have an ongoing riddle or puzzle of the day or week, with the first person to solve it earning recognition—a loud gong, a flashing light, a free lunch, or 50 percent discount on your own products or services?

Can you make a contest of your work? Think up silly tricks or techniques and gather a prize pool of white elephants from coworkers who bought too much in a garage sale and use these to reward successful contestants?

If you put your mind to it, you or someone you work with can probably think of ways to bring fun to work. Fun will make you more productive—not to mention popular.

TIME FOR A CHECKUP

When's the last time you had a hilarious laugh at work?

Do you have access to cartoons or joke books?

Are you waiting for someone else to entertain or amuse you?

MOVE FROM LEFT-BRAIN TO RIGHT-BRAIN ACTIVITIES

Just as eating against one's will is injurious to health, so study without a liking for it spoils the memory, and it retains nothing it takes in.—LEONARDO DA VINCI

Recognizing your current brain activity and switching to the other brain hemisphere increases your energy for a new project. Unlimited energy comes from learning to integrate and balance activities from both sides of your brain in any given work period.

LEFT-BRAIN ACTIVITIES	RIGHT-BRAIN ACTIVITIES
Investigating a situation	Investigating a hunch about a person
Gathering facts	Creating visuals to use in a presentation
Reading technical information	Expressing thanks to a coworker for good job
Writing a report or letter	Interviewing a job candidate
Repairing equipment	Taking an oral survey

Creating a system	Experimenting with a new piece of equipment
Organizing a project	Giving constructive feedback to a boss
Calculating figures	Planning your strategy with a new prospect
Drafting policy	Scouting out new property to buy

In addition to having more energy, you'll think and learn about a project in a different way. If you're stumped on a project, try to pick it up at a different point. For a change of pace, can you change projects altogether?

If you work all day at a computer, do something more physically taxing in the evening like cabinetry. If you work on your feet all day, then plan a relaxing evening playing some computer games.

Most of us have a preference for one brain dominance. Do you know your preference at work? At home? Striking a balance between both kinds of activities can produce the most creative results and satisfying emotion.

Time for a Checkup

Try to categorize your typical tasks as either left-brain or right-brain activities. Does your day provide enough latitude to move from one hemisphere to the other?

Do your off-work activities give you a chance to think from the opposite side of your brain—or are your at-home pursuits just "more of the same"?

THINK
RATIONALLY

Time is the only thing we use faster than money.—UNKNOWN

You may march to a different drummer, but should you speed up or slow down the beat?—DIANNA BOOHER

Are the goals, pace, and schedules you've set for yourself reasonable? Even possible?

When a staff member comes to me feeling overwhelmed, we sit down together to do a task audit and priority check. The first thing I usually notice is a list of to-do's scheduled for the current week.

"When do you think you'll have these finished?" I ask.

"I don't know—this week, I hope. I'm working as fast as I can. I know they have to be done."

"How long will this project A take?" I ask.

"I don't know. Maybe five to six hours."

"How long will this project B take?"

"I think maybe a day—two days at most."

"How long will this project C take?"

"That should go pretty fast. Couple of hours."

"How long will this project D take?"

"That's gonna take some work—maybe three days, if things go well."

"And are you planning to finish all these this week?"

"I'm going to try."

No wonder that staffer feels pressured and over-whelmed. The projects he just ticked off—if they all go as well as estimated—will require six and a quarter days, not counting interruptions for the unexpected. He works a five-day week.

When you're feeling overwhelmed, remind yourself to think rationally. Is it humanly possible to get done all the projects you've scheduled for yourself? Are there enough hours in the day?

Think bigger. What demands have you set for your-self as a parent? Professional? Spouse? Adult son or daughter? Citizen? Is it rational to think that any per-son, given the best of circumstances and talents, could meet all the demands?

If not, be reasonable. Make an accurate assessment of what you can do, and download or postpone the rest. Keeping those duties dangling in front of you will ensure that you never feel the satisfaction of accom-plishment and always feel the frustration of being over-whelmed.

Time for a Checkup

Have you converted your to-do list to actual hours?

Will the hours required for your typical work tasks fit into the amount of time you're on the job?

Will the hours for your personal responsibilities and plans fit into your waking hours at home?

KNOW WHY YOU'RE DOING WHAT YOU'RE DOING SO YOU KNOW WHEN TO STOP DOING IT

Counting time is not so important as making time count.
— JAMES WALKER

According to time expert Hyrum Smith, when people feel out of control, it is because they have lost sight of "why." Activities often become meaningless in and of themselves when we lose sight of the purpose—what we hoped to accomplish in the bigger scheme of things.

Take gardening, for example. If you feel as if weeds are overtaking the entire patch and that you're spending every last minute running to the nursery to buy insecticide to spray for some new kind of vermin, you may grow weary with the garden. The garden has become a demand on your time. The garden has become an end in itself.

But if you remember that you planted the garden because you wanted a chance to get outside on Saturdays for a change of pace from your normal office routine, that you actually feel soothed emotionally when you see green plants from your window, that you enjoy the fresh tomatoes on your table, then you feel reenergized for the gardening tasks.

If you don't feel renewed energy when you recall the why behind a task or activity, then your reasons have evaporated. Your goals have changed. Your likes or needs have disappeared. You can stop doing the activity.

TIME FOR A CHECKUP

Do you have office procedures that have outlived their usefulness to get the job done?

Have some of your hobbies become work?

Do you still try to find time to visit places that you no longer enjoy?

Are you working at learning a new skill that you no longer think you need?

Are you seeing people socially who bore you?

DUMP UNREALISTIC EXPECTATIONS AND MYTHS

Time is not a road—it is a room.—JOHN FOWLES

Returning from a National Speakers Association convention several years ago, I sat on the plane listening to an audiotape of Pat Vivo's keynote speech. She was relating her moving story about growing up in a home with both parents deaf. My husband tapped me on the shoulder: "Why are you crying?"

"She's so good."

"You're crying because she's so good?"

"No, I'm crying because . . . I can't ever be that good—I can't ever move people like that. I don't have a tragedy in my past."

"Let me get this straight—you're crying because you don't have a *tragedy* in your life."

"Not exactly. I'm depressed because I'm never going to be able to motivate people by telling about some great obstacle I overcame. I can't move people emotionally."

Being an inspirational speaker with such a powerfully moving personal story was an unrealistic burden

I'd placed on myself when beginning my career as a speaker in the corporate world. And what's more, I've decided I don't want to have to experience tragedy to have a motivating keynote.

You have to dump unrealistic expectations of yourself about what you can accomplish—or be—in a day or in a lifetime.

TIME FOR A CHECKUP

Are you living your life's goals, or those of your parents or spouse?

Have people frequently told you that you have your head in the clouds?

Do people routinely comment to you, "You're too hard on yourself."

REFUSE TO OVERCOMMIT YOURSELF

Unless he manages himself effectively, no amount of ability, skill, experience or knowledge will make an executive effective.—Peter Drucker

Some people cannot say no because their self-esteem comes from the feeling of being needed. As long as someone is asking them to share their efficiency, skills, talents, or time, they feel good about themselves.

Time is a high price to pay for self-esteem.

If you're tempted to take on more than you can realistically handle, ask yourself these two questions: "Does this activity fit my goals and values?" "Why am I being asked to do this task—because no one else has the expertise, or because no one else will say yes?" If you don't like the answers to these questions, pass up the "opportunity."

Some people overcommit themselves because they just can't word a firm no—to bosses, to peers, to family, to friends. If you have difficulty getting no out of your mouth when someone seems to have a real need and a good cause, think of the no in a positive way: Think of the no to one thing as a yes to something else. Instead of saying, "No, I can't do X," try, "I've decided to devote all my time and attention to Y." Focus the conversation on what you have decided *to commit to* rather than on what you have decided *not to commit to*.

Some people take on more than they can do because they enjoy or are comfortable with being a victim and having ready excuses for not excelling or not getting things done. These people think: "Okay, I'm braced—whatever hits first gets my attention."

Do you really want to let happenstance or others dictate your priorities?

Time for a Checkup

Are you now involved in a volunteer project for which you have no personal enthusiasm?

Why were you asked to take on this project?

Why did you accept this project?

LEARN TO SAY NO TO DUTIFUL TO-DO'S

Time is the only coin you have in life...and only you can determine how it will be spent. Be careful lest you let other people spend it for you.—CARL SANDBURG

Own less, do less, say no.—GEOFFREY GODBEY

I'm not necessarily talking drudgery here. Several weekends ago, I reminded my husband that we needed to get tickets for the state fair because the upcoming weekend was the last weekend when we'd both be in town before the fair ended. He nodded agreement. But as we got closer to Saturday, I noticed that he didn't mention the event with his usual enthusiasm. Nevertheless, despite the growing to-do list for my own weekend, I phoned my daughter and son-in-law to ask to ask if they would be free to join us. When she responded that they already had plans for the day, I reported that to my husband.

"Well, if you change your mind about the fair and decide you'd rather be shopping for wallpaper, that's okay by me."

"You don't mind if we don't go?" I asked, surprised.

"Actually, I was wanting to draw sketches for my new garage shelves."

Easy decision—we skipped the fair.

But how many other social or business obligations have we "performed" because one or the other of us thought we *should*—like attending the neighborhood crime-watch meeting to have input into how they organize the blocks. Like accepting an invitation to a client open-house after work. Like attending the wedding of the cousin of the aunt of the coworker we see only once a month. Like attending the recital of the child next door. Like cooking a gourmet meal for the couple who invited us for dinner last year where we drove two hours to get to their house and had no common interest with any other guest.

Learn to be honest with yourself and others by deciding not to fill your calendar with low-priority obligations.

Time for a Checkup

Do you accept invitations to social functions that you don't actually enjoy?

Do you listen to people's problems when you know you can't help them and know they don't really want help?

Do you go to club meetings when you're sick?

Do you send gifts for occasions when you don't really know the people involved?

Do you donate money to causes just because someone asked you and because everyone else seems to be donating?

DROP PROFESSIONAL ORGANIZATIONS THAT ARE SHOULDS

> *If people are highly successful in their profession they lose their senses. Sight goes. They have no time to look at pictures. Sound goes. They have no time to listen to music. Speech goes. They have no time for conversation. They lose their sense of proportion—the relations between one and another. Humanity goes.*
> —VIRGINIA WOOLF, *Three Guineas*

Drop professional organizations that are "obligatory" but not beneficial.

Equate them with PR to determine their worth. People involved in getting media exposure (ad agencies and corporate public relationships departments) will tell you to keep your name in front of people if you expect to sell them a product or service. However, these PR specialists will also tell you that their clients or CEOs are forever pressing them with this bottom-line question: Is the PR actually bringing customers through our doors? Can we really trace product and service sales to that media exposure?

Think of membership in professional organizations

in the same way: Sure, they have some benefit to your career—if nothing more than your picking up a new idea from the luncheon speaker or networking with a specific colleague who tells you where to find a good printer. But the question should be: What *specific* benefits can you trace to that membership? Has membership ever gotten you a better job assignment? Has membership ever been instrumental in getting you a raise? Has membership ever brought business through your door? Is membership actually making you a better leader, engineer, or financial planner?

At one point in my career, I belonged to eight professional associations (as a writer, speaker, consultant, trainer). When I found myself dreading those calls for volunteer assignments, I decided I had to either get active or get out. The current list has become very short—less time with higher payoff.

Do a real-time-versus-benefit analysis. Question whether the time, money, and guilt (of not taking on additional committee responsibilities) is worth the effort.

Time for a Checkup

Do you dread going to the meetings?

Are the meetings and related camaraderie a refreshing break from a monotonous daily job?

What dollar value can you put on your investment of time in extracurricular assignments for the organization?

SKIP HOLIDAY HASSLES

Holidays: a period of activity so intense that it can only be undertaken three or four weeks in the year.—MILES KINGTON, "A Guide to Real Meanings," *The London Times*, February 7, 1983.

Why do people look so gloomy in January? They're exhausted from all the holiday hoopla. The cooking, cleaning, shopping, decorating, partying, cards, visitors, gift returns, rehearsals, and programs.

Our spirits sour the season when we're skimming from one activity to the next just to get everything done. For many families, holidays mean being with extended families that they don't enjoy (or even dislike) and spending money for things they can't afford. Both of which lead to depression and an increased financial burden when January arrives.

You notice I didn't say skip the fun, rest, or spirit of the holidays—only the hassles. For the last several years, our extended family has opted for meeting at the mall, pooling our family gift-giving money, and donating it for a needy family (paying their rent for a month, taking them a tree, and buying gifts for their kids). Not only have we cut down on our family shopping time, but we've had a chance to spend time together as a family and do a little good for someone else.

On one Thanksgiving occasion, our extended family gathered in a resort area for a few days of fun without the work. We ate our Thanksgiving meal at a local restaurant buffet and then spent the afternoon watching football in front of the fireplace and walking off lunch among the deer in the surrounding wooded areas. Time to talk, play games, enjoy each other—with none of the associated work.

If you're dreading the holidays because of the hassles, consider simplifying the system. Announce your decision early to your family so they can make adjustments in their plans. Then focus on the spiritual significance and forget all the meaningless, tiresome trappings.

TIME FOR A CHECKUP

Do you send the same photocopied letter or card (rather than a personal note) to all the people on your Christmas list?

Are you buying desserts rather than making them?

Are you relieved or sad when your holiday company goes home?

Do you have to "take a few days off" to rest after a major holiday?

Do you feel depressed or overwhelmed during or before the holiday even begins?

DON'T DRESS
TO THE NINES
IF YOU CAN
WEAR NIKES

A group of men in evening clothes looks like a flock of crows, and is just about as inspiring.—MARK TWAIN

Clothes often fake the man.—ANONYMOUS

Some people dress to kill, others just want to hurt us.
—ANONYMOUS

I timed myself one morning to discover it was taking me thirty-five minutes to do my hair. Then looking at the circles under my eyes, I decided that another thirty-five minutes of sleep would have done more for my appearance than the hairdo. I got a simpler cut and style.

Teenage girls often complain (brag?) about how long it takes them to get dressed for a date. The nails. The hair. The four changes of clothes. Finding the right belt and earrings. Changing purses. But do you still have time for that kind of thing as an adult?

For many people, it's not so much changing the way they style their hair or the clothes they wear; the time-consuming part is the actual act of getting dressed in the morning. Try on this. No, that looks too wrinkled. Try on that. No, somebody borrowed my belt and didn't return it. Polish those nails. Oops, smudged them.

Start over. Pull the white shirt off the rack and then discover the cuff button is missing. Try on the blazer. No, doesn't look good with those slacks. Will this tie go? No, here's the tie I need, but it has gravy stains on the front. Sound familiar?

Organize your closet and bureau so you can find things easily. If something needs to be mended, cleaned, or washed, don't return it to the closet where you'll grab it again without remembering the problem. Everything works better with a system—even dressing and grooming. Simplify your system—and your look—so you don't have to think in the morning.

Know the best colors and styles for your coloring and frame and then build your entire wardrobe around a few quality items. (You'll save money on this principle, too, by eliminating impulse buys that don't "go" with anything else.)

Try the simple-but-elegant approach.

Time for a Checkup

How much time do you spend in personal grooming every day? In the average week?

Could you close your eyes and pull any garment out of your closet and find it in wearable condition?

How many times in the typical week day or weekend do you change clothes, accessories, makeup, and shoes?

How many minutes do you spend matching garments and accessories before you can pull an outfit together?

LAUNDRY LATER

After Ecstasy, the laundry.—Anonymous Zen Statement

As a teenager when I did the laundry for our family, we wore everyday clothes until they got dirty. Sometimes that meant I wore a sweater and jeans every afternoon after school from 4:00 p.m. to bedtime for three or four days running. We wore the same play clothes Saturday and Sunday. Then we did the laundry once a week and started over.

Now, after wearing a pair of sweats to take a 45-minute walk, I toss them in the clothes hamper.

My grandmother changed the sheets on all the beds every week. My mother changed the sheets on all the beds every week. Like clockwork, I changed the sheets on every bed every week. Until one day it dawned on me that I was changing sheets weekly when I often spent only one or two nights at home rather than in a hotel room. Why? Habit.

A washer and dryer in every home has reduced the scrub and rinse time, but increased the total time we spend doing laundry—sorting, carrying, loading, bleaching/spraying, unloading, folding, putting away.

Can you cut down the amount of laundry by using the same towel for two or three baths? Wearing the same jeans more than once? Running in the same jogging socks two days? A washer load here and a washer load there (and all the related tasks) turn laundry into the same kind of time-consuming task your great-grandmother did on Mondays from dawn to dusk.

And for those clothes that need to be dry-cleaned, you're spending even more time on the road and wasting more mental energy to remember to drop them off and pick them up. Keep any purchases that dictate dry-cleaning to a minimum.

Before you change clothes, towels, or sheets, remember that laundry involves more than dropping clothes in the washer and pushing the button.

TIME FOR A CHECKUP

How many times do you change clothes every day?

Are you doing more or fewer wash loads per week than you were a decade ago?

Is every family member washer-and-dryer-literate enough to do his or her own laundry?

CLEAN ONLY WHAT YOU NEED TO CLEAN

AND WHEN YOU NEED TO CLEAN

Cleaning anything involves making something else dirty, but anything can get dirty without something else getting clean.
—DR. LAURENCE J. PETER

Like laundry, cleaning multiplies. You've heard the old time axiom, "Tasks expand according to the time allotted for them." Nowhere is that truer than with cleaning chores. I can clean my home in two hours or twenty hours, depending. . . . (Not depending on how dirty, but depending on how much time I have.)

Why clean the baseboards every week? Who inspects them and how often? Why dust the bookcases every week? Do you have guests who do the white-glove test on the corner of your shelves? Granted, bathrooms and kitchens generally warrant a good cleaning every week, but other chores are optional for most households.

Keep these four principles in mind:

1. *Clean only what you need to clean.* We do a lot of entertaining, and I wouldn't think of having company for dinner without vacuuming. But why vacuum the week I *know* no one but my spouse and I will set foot inside our house?

2. *Clean only when you need to clean it.* Why mop the entire floor if you have only one splash of tea under the table? Just mop or wipe up the tea stain.

3. *Have all the tools you need* (cleaners, rags, brushes, mops) *in one* carrier. Move the bucket, basket, pouch, or tray with you as you work your way from room to room.

4. *For the huge cleaning projects* (like washing windows, cleaning the garage, vacuuming the upholstery and drapes) *that need to be done only a few times a year, hire someone by the hour.* Call the local high school or college for help.

I learned these four principles in the last twelve months. My cleaning lady retired about two weeks before I was to leave for a long trip out of the country. So I decided to wait until we returned to hire a replacement. But before I could start the search, my real estate agent called to say she had a prospect to look at the house. Though I didn't have time to clean, vacuum, mop, or dust that morning before work, I okayed the house showing anyway. Result? The agent called to say, "The house showed beautifully and we have an interested buyer."

The house couldn't have been that dirty, then, right? I delayed my cleaning-service search another week. More agents and buyers—all with the same feedback after the showing, "Your house shows like a new home—so well kept." Obviously, free-of-clutter passes for clean with most people. Keeping stuff in its proper place will make real cleanups fewer and quicker.

The "spot" cleaning principle works. Clean only what is really dirty and only when you need it to be clean.

With the house well organized and things in their proper place, you can go a lot longer between *real* cleaning days.

TIME FOR A CHECKUP

Do you mop floors even when you can see no stains there?

Do you vacuum every room in the house every week—whether the rooms have had traffic or not?

Do you dust everything every week—even if you've had no sandstorm and you're not expecting visitors?

Can you look around the house and diagnose the problem—disaster or dirt? (They require different solutions.)

SHOP LIKE YOU DON'T MEAN IT

Fortunate, indeed, is the man who takes exactly the right measure of himself, and holds a just balance between what he can acquire and what he can use.—PETER LATHAM

Like cleaning, shopping is one of those chores that can easily expand to fill the time allotted. (I'm not talking about the shopping-as-an-entertainment activity here, but shopping for essential items to keep the household running—groceries, toilet paper, school supplies, tennis shoes, mufflers.)

To quote the motivational speaker Zig Ziglar in his sales seminars, consider cost, not price. Don't stop with just looking at the price tag; consider the total time, effort, energy, and mileage something costs from start to finish in selecting your purchases.

These guidelines will help:

- Shop in places near where you live.
- Shop in stores that are familiar, where you know where to find things. A supermarket "on the way" some place may be quick to enter, but you may spend fifteen minutes searching for the few items you need.
- Shop in stores that have ample staff on hand to answer questions, exchange merchandise, and take

your money without requiring you to stand in long lines.

- Map a route for the shopping trip rather than make haphazard jaunts.
- Bunch routine errands for one time slot.
- Shop at off hours. (Don't go to the grocery store around noon on Saturday!)
- Buy in bulk.
- Never run out of any staple item. Always keep a supply on hand.
- Look at your calendar for the next week or month and notice the "special" items you need—birthday cards, gifts, ingredients for potluck dishes, school lunches.
- Shop by mail—unless the items are clothes that may not fit and will require time and effort in returning them.
- Select gifts that you can buy from home and have delivered or mailed (almost anything nowadays).
- Get acquainted with store personnel who know what you like in furniture, clothes, collectibles, and so forth and ask them to call you when shipments that may interest you come in. (You don't have to run to the store just because they call.)
- Use a personal shopper.

Consider the total cost of purchases—price, gas, time, turmoil.

TIME FOR A CHECKUP

How many trips to the grocery store do you make in the typical week?

Do you frequently run out of staple items—flour, toothpaste, soap, hosiery, stationery?

Do you dart back and forth across town to buy things "on sale"?

Are you surprised by upcoming events, causing you to make special shopping trips at inconvenient times to buy gifts or specialty items?

SIMPLIFY YOUR RECORDKEEPING

Life's been nothing but paperwork.—GUSTAVE MAHLER

You won't eat less beef today, because you have written down what it cost yesterday.—SAMUEL JOHNSON, quoted by James Boswell in *Life of Samuel Johnson*, 1791.

Granted, the government shoulders much of the blame for our paperwork hassles. But we ourselves complicate things in several ways. For every checking and savings account you open, you'll need to reconcile end-of-the-month statements. For every investment account you open, you'll have monthly or quarterly statements. For every credit card you use, you have monthly statements. For every trust fund you set up, you have statements and tax reports. For every magazine, you'll have a subscription to pay, renew, forward, or cancel. For your possessions, you'll need to buy insurance policies and make payments. For medical visits, you have insurance forms to file, payments to make, end-of-year reconciliations, and the resulting deductions or income for your tax reports. The list goes on.

To consolidate and eliminate recordkeeping, write all your checks from one checking account. If you have other accounts for savings but write no checks from them, the recordkeeping will be much simpler.

For investment purposes, buy into two or three fund families and keep your money diversified by switching funds within these two or three families. Any financial planner will tell you that the issue is not timing the market but time in the market. Select solid investments and stay put for the long haul.

If you have a choice about HMOs and other medical options, consider the paperwork time involved before deciding on the best option for your family.

Put all your purchases on one or two major credit cards. Keep the others only to establish a good record and to bail yourself out of real emergencies. You'll eliminate writing checks to so many different companies at the end of the month. For magazine subscriptions, keep all your receipts and expiration dates in one place.

As a general rule, shop for turnkey operations in buying products and services. If you have flood damage to your house, instead of dealing with a carpet company, a furniture company, a carpentry shop, and a painter, look for a general contractor who can handle all the repairs, deal with all the different vendors, do the follow-up, pay the bills, and keep the records.

And do invest in a good software package that does all the balancing and tracking for you. Yes, it'll take three to four hours to get all your data entered, but thereafter your recordkeeping will be much faster and simpler—without having to sacrifice good financial overviews or accuracy.

TIME FOR A CHECKUP

Do you balance your checking and savings accounts each month, or play catch-up about every three months?

Could a relative or friend, in case of emergency, check your financial records and know how to keep your household running?

Do you have difficulty in knowing whether to buy or sell investments at the end of the year because you don't have a clue about your cost basis and the tax implications?

Are you paying annual credit card fees on cards that you don't use?

Does the time you spend in recordkeeping exceed the earnings on your investments?

REMEMBER THAT PLANTS AREN'T NECESSARILY LIVING THINGS

Plant and your spouse plants with you, weed and you weed alone.—DENIS BREEZE

(If you love working with plants, lawn, and garden and find living things relieve stress or provide an emotional lift, skip this chapter. Otherwise, read on.)

I love live plants. Connecting with nature nourishes the soul. But growing plants takes tender loving care. Watering. Feeding. Trimming falling (dying, in *my* house) leaves. Drying water splashed on window sills or carpets. Vacuuming dirt that falls overboard with the brown or yellow leaves. Removing stains from the carpet after moving the pots. Doctoring them for bugs. Dusting the cobwebs from them. Replacing dead plants. Moving them toward or away from the light.

And then there's the lawn, garden, and flower beds. Mowing. Edging. Bagging and dumping clippings. Watering. Fertilizing. Spraying with pesticides. Trimming. Raking. Weeding. Maintaining and repairing the lawn and gardening equipment.

Living things take time.

Consider enjoying live plants by walking outdoors along the street or park and keeping only artificial plants inside. Consider landscaping with sand, dirt, or sawdust trails, rocks, sculpture, or any of a number of ground covers with no maintenance. Or consider marrying a spouse who has the time and patience to provide the plant care that you need!

TIME FOR A CHECKUP

How many hours per month do you spend working on your lawn or garden?

How many hours do you spend outside enjoying your lawn or garden?

Are your houseplants attractive and decorative in their current condition?

TURN OFF THE TELEVISION

The unfortunate thing about this world is that good habits are so much easier to give up than bad ones.—SOMERSET MAUGHAM

When my children reached school age, we decided that there would be no television on weekdays. By omitting this option from their schedule, we hoped to encourage them to get more exercise outdoors, spend more time reading, do more thorough homework, interact more often with friends on the phone and in stayovers, participate in the dinnertime conversation a little longer, and take part in more afterschool extracurricular activities. Results: all the above.

From first grade through high school, they never really missed television—never even argued about it. On the few occasions they did watch TV on weeknights because of a history or English assignment, they considered it a special event.

Because they didn't watch TV, we as parents didn't watch TV. Result: We weren't enticed by all the advertising to spend more than we could afford. And we haven't become aware of any role models we or the kids missed for our lives.

Television is a time-consuming addiction.

TIME FOR A CHECKUP

How many hours a week do you watch television?

How many hours would someone have to devote to gambling or drinking before you'd label it an addiction?

What are the benefits of TV in your life?

Do you feel particularly educated, inspired, motivated, rested, or happy after an evening of television?

Which provides more food for thought or fodder for a conversation—a weekly TV episode or a popular book?

COMMUNICATE CLEARLY THE FIRST TIME

The greatest problem in communication is the illusion that it has been accomplished.—GEORGE BERNARD SHAW

It takes two to speak the truth—one to speak and another to hear.—HENRY DAVID THOREAU

We hardly have time to tell people things the first time, much less time to tell them over and over. And over. And to straighten up the foul-ups caused by inadvertent miscommunications. These guidelines should help:

Be direct.   Don't couch an opinion or objection in a question. Don't ask, "Do you think that vendor can meet our deadline?" and expect the listener to read your mind. Instead, *say,* "I don't think that vendor can meet our deadline."

Overview first; then elaborate.   Summarize "the point," then go back and fill in the details as necessary.

Be specific rather than general.   Not: "I need this as soon as possible." But: "I need this by Friday noon." Not: "We don't handle that sort of thing in this office." But: "We don't handle the amortization schedules in this office."

Use concrete words and phrases.   Not: "We need
your cooperation to cut expenses." But: "We need
you to make sure the lights and air-conditioning are
off when you leave for the day."

State the do's along with the don'ts: Not: "Do not
force the lever when jammed." So does the user say
"pretty please" to get the machine to work? Try:
"When the lever jams, press the release button. If
that doesn't work, call us for service."

Listen.   Listening is not waiting your turn to speak.
Listening requires your undivided attention to the
speaker's facts, feelings, and conclusions about
those facts and feelings shared.

Verify assumptions.   Someone says to you, "The
insurance coverage here is not what I'm used to at
my previous place of business." Possible interpreta-
tions: The coverage here is better. The coverage here
is worse. The deductible is higher. The deductible is
lower. My payments are now higher. I'm glad I don't
have to come up with such big payments here. I
don't have coverage for the medical procedures my
family members need. I don't understand how to
complete the claims form. I don't like the amount of
paperwork involved. I'm surprised at the prompt
payment of my claims. And so on.

Double-check the facts.   Did John say the merchandise was damaged *when* it arrived on the dock—or
that the merchandise was damaged *after* it was
delivered—or that the merchandise was defective
before it was even shipped? Did Joan say they *prefer*
payment by credit card—or that payment by credit
card was *acceptable*?

Lead discussions if you're in charge.   Endless hours are wasted in circular conversations—in meetings, in the hallway, at home. If you "own" the meeting or conversation, take charge.

Solicit information, opinions, and feelings before acting.   Make sure you can (and want to) enforce what you say before you say it. Generally, you're on safer ground if you ask for input before you make a decision or take action rather than after you make a decision or take action.

Sell, don't just tell.   Even if you're in charge and have the final say, sell your ideas. Things happen faster and better when other people "buy in" to your plans rather than sabotage them.

Summarize lengthy conversations.   Minds wander. Memory fails. After an important conversation, summarize what you said and heard. That may be your last chance for clarity.

Clarify who is to do what next.   "These procedures really need to be reviewed before the next project comes along." Who's going to do that? Are you sure?

Be courteous and show respect.   Stay away from hot words, emotional words, accusations, judgmental labels, sarcasm. When you make people angry, you may "make a point," but do you have time to deal with the fallout?

Say it clearly the first time.

TIME FOR A CHECKUP

How often do you have to send people reminders and explanations after you have already sent out a memo, letter, or E-mail that you thought was perfectly clear to begin with?

How often do others ask for clarification after you speak or write?

How often do people not carry out directives you consider clear and straightforward?

When you give instructions on projects, do you generally get the results you want?

LEARN WHEN AND HOW TO TERMINATE CIRCULAR CONVERSATIONS

> *A good memory and a tongue tied in the middle is a combination which gives immortality to conversation.*—MARK TWAIN

Some people have been having the same conversations for a lifetime. They tell you about their terrible place of work. They give you a weekly rundown on their love affair that's in jeopardy. They ask for, but never take, advice on a new business venture.

If such conversations take valuable time and sap your emotional energy, try to focus these repetitive, rambling speakers by asking questions. "So what do you think the next step should be?" "So what specifically do you want me to do at this point?" "So what do you plan to do now?" "So how have things/your plans/the relationship changed? Is this something different from what we've discussed before?"

If such questions don't help them focus and come to resolution, you may want to be more direct: "Gee, I'd really like to be able to offer some help, but I've exhausted all my ideas on the situation." Or: "I really empathize with your situation. And I wish I could say something to help. I'm beginning to become as emotionally involved and upset about the situation as you are. Do you mind if we change the subject?"

If the conversation is one in which someone repeatedly asks your advice but doesn't take it, you can try: "What did you decide to do about the last bit of advice I passed along?" "I'm afraid you won't find my current advice any more usable than what I offered last time we talked." Or: "I'm sorry but I really don't have any more ideas (am fresh out of new ideas) about the situation/issue."

If necessary, say it again. And again.

Time for a Checkup

Are you becoming a "counselor" to a friend or coworker who has problems bigger than you feel qualified to handle?

Do you feel depressed or drained after conversations with this person?

Are you really helping the person going in circles, or simply delaying his or her getting to the real source and resolution for the issue/problem? Can you offer another source for help or information?

TUNE OUT KIDS' ROUTINE BELLYACHIN'

How long a minute is depends on which side of the bathroom door you're on.—ANONYMOUS

A good parent must like his children, but he must not have an urgent need to be liked by them every minute of the day.
—HAIM GINOTT, M.D.

The two most difficult careers are entrusted to amateurs—citizenship and parenthood.—ANONYMOUS

Very few things can be as emotionally draining as hearing kids whine and complain and feel that somehow you as parent are responsible to entertain or referee them. Lest you think only *your* household is stunting children's emotional growth and future happiness, be reassured that the following comments can be heard in kitchens across America:

Why can't I?

But Dad/Mom said I could.

All the other kids' parents let them.

Don't you trust me?

But you said I could the next time—and this is the next time.

But you always get to . . .

Why do you keep treating me like a baby?

I'm just a kid—why do I have to . . .

I'm busy—why do I have to do it now?

I'll do it later.

You told me already.

I didn't know I was supposed to do that.

Why does she (or he) get away with it and I don't?

Why don't you make her (or him) do it?

Why did he (or she) get more than me?

He (or she) won't leave me alone.

He (or she) won't give it back.

Make him (or her) get out of my room/leave my stuff alone/get off my computer.

Why don't I get a bigger allowance?

She (or he) doesn't have to spend her (or his) allowance on things like that.

It only costs $20.

All the other parents buy their kids stuff like that all the time.

Are you going to wear that—oooh, I'll be so embarrassed.

I'm going to run away.

Why didn't you come get me earlier?

I don't love you anymore.

Can you bring me a drink of water, please?

Yuck—are we having that again?

Everybody else is going.

So why do I have to call? There won't be any phones.

Nobody's parents make them do that anymore.

Filter these comments from your psyche, and do not let them produce guilt or defensiveness. As much as possible, explain your reasoning and then set your limits or state your decisions. Teach your kids to talk and reason without whining (listen only when the whine disappears). Encourage them to mediate their own petty disagreements—with incentives for both sides for early resolutions that do not involve you as arbitrator.

Show them that you can listen—without becoming defensive, retaliating, or changing your mind.

Your kids will turn into great human beings after they pass the age of about eighteen and once again take responsibility for their own daily to-do's and difficulties.

TIME FOR A CHECKUP

Do you take responsibility for refereeing petty disagreements between your kids?

Do you feel guilty when your kids tell you "everybody else is"?

Do you feel manipulated by your kids?

What other information sources can you develop so that you can gain an unbiased perspective on norms for other households (what kind of parties Julie has, what time the local teen hangout closes, what policies go unenforced at school, a suitable allowance for lunch money)?

GET RID OF THE GRUMPS IN YOUR LIFE

Depend upon it that if a man talks of his misfortunes there is something in them that is not disagreeable to him, for where there is nothing but pure misery there never is any recourse to the mention of it.—Samuel Johnson, quoted by J. Boswell in *Life of Johnson.*

I don't believe in the goodness of disagreeable people.
—O. Dewey

Negative people sap your energy and attention. They break your focus. I used to have an employee—I'll call her Gertrude—who wouldn't speak before nine. When she walked in in the morning, it was "grrrhhh"—if she was in a reasonable mood. If we closed the office for a holiday, it was the wrong holiday, according to her—one that she would have rather worked so she could have taken another day. If we decided to order in Chinese for somebody's birthday, she wanted barbecue. I'd congratulate her and a coworker for doing a great job on a project, and she'd write me a note telling me the coworker hadn't helped all that much. She just wanted to "set the record straight."

I put up with this disposition and attitude for about three years because she was a very productive employee.

But one day, she came in and presented a...challenge for me. Could she start working part-time? "I really want to work about 30 hours a week—just to be at home when my kids leave for school and when they get home. I don't need the insurance because I can get on my husband's policy. Could we just pro-rate everything else—the retirement, the vacation days, the holidays, and so forth?"

I agreed. She could work the number of hours she wanted, come in and leave when she wanted, take the vacations or holidays she wanted. She loved me—for about three weeks. Then she caught me at the copier one morning. "My husband doesn't want me on his insurance policy. So I need to get back on yours."

"No," I told her, "we don't provide insurance for part-time employees. That wasn't part of your original request."

"Then I'll be looking for another job immediately." She turned on her heel and stalked away.

The next day, she had a note on my desk. "I want to keep working full-time. Please ignore what I said yesterday. In no way did I offer my resignation."

Okay. So I waited. Two days later she had another note in my in-box. "I've changed my mind. I want to work 28 hours a week. Nine to 2:30. I'll pay my own insurance. . . . And if you'll okay this arrangement, I'll agree to work here for one more year."

I called her into my office again. "Gertrude, you can work whatever and whenever you want to here, but I'd encourage you to go ahead and begin your job search. I wouldn't think of holding you here for another year."

That has been one of the best employee decisions I've ever made.

You can teach someone skills, but you can't teach them attitude and disposition. And negative people have a way of drenching your whole office or home in a downpour. Negative people drain your energy and your time and break your concentration on the important things.

TIME FOR A CHECKUP

Who are the negative people at work?

Who are the negative people in your personal life—family members, neighbors, club acquaintances?

How many hours of sleep have you lost over situations involving this person?

How can you minimize necessary contact with these people?

FIND SOUL
MATES AT WORK

I always try to balance the light with the heavy—a few tears of human spirit in with the sequins and the fringes.
—BETTE MIDLER

Whatever our souls are made of, his and mine are the same.
—EMILY BRONTE, *Wuthering Heights*, 1847

Pleasant people lift your spirit. One of our employees this past year placed a valentine heart and Snoopy greeting card on everyone's desk. Wouldn't you rather work for, with, beside, manage, or lead someone with that kind of disposition and attitude? Do those people energize you? To quote Mark Hansen and Jack Canfield, that's chicken soup for the soul.

You may be working so hard that you've lost your emotional bearings on the job. Even the most task-oriented people (and I'm one of those) need emotional connections with others. Find people at work who know your strengths and weaknesses, who know the culture you work in, and who encourage as well as commiserate with you.

TIME FOR A CHECKUP

Who are the family members who always encourage you in new ventures? Have you developed the same kind of friendships at work?

Do you have someone at work that you'd feel comfortable telling about an impending divorce?

Do you have someone with whom you could discuss a moral conflict on the job?

Do you have someone at work who understands the stresses you experience from a supervisor, an employee, a vendor, a customer, or a team?

Who at work would care deeply if your parent or child were seriously ill?

Do you have a confidant at work who would be happy for you (rather than jealous) if you received a promotion over him or her?

If you don't have those kinds of friends at work, have you devoted the time to show concern in similar situations?

GET EMOTIONAL SUPPORT FROM PERSONAL RELATIONSHIPS

In choosing career over family what's going out the window is the whole dynamic of caring. Often, we just don't have time to show how much we care.—RAY BARDILL

Work relationships cannot take the place of personal relationships apart from the office—marriage, family, friends. That commonality of friendships developed at work generally has a way of keeping workplace problems or issues in the forefront of your conversations, your activities, and your time together. And that focus in itself keeps you teetering off balance and uncentered.

First, take time for your family. Try not to get caught up in the routine of routine activities—just going through the rituals of living together without connecting with each other emotionally and without enjoying each other. Take time to eat meals together. Take time to travel together. Schedule some fun activities together. If nothing else, run errands together so that you have time to talk during activities that are not mentally taxing.

Second, consider the priority your marriage or a love relationship and family hold in your life: (1) marriage and family above both careers, (2) husband's career above wife's career, (3) wife's career above husband's, (4) both careers above the marriage and family. If you find yourself disagreeing about any of the priority situations or if you're definitely in situation 4, you will experience increasing stress and emotional unbalance. Talk over such an imbalance. If you don't like what you discover, consider these changes:

- One spouse works outside the home only part-time.
- One spouse finds a job with flexible work hours.
- One spouse finds a job to allow working from home.
- Both partners reduce their career goals.
- Both partners reduce their standard of living and/or cut expenses.

Once you've decided on the most workable schedule, hours, and commitment, then make some mental accommodations to offer each other emotional support as the most intimate of all teams. Here are some guidelines that have worked in my own marriage:

- Decide who does what best and let that person do those related tasks.
- Capitalize on the "opposites attract" personalities. If you're easily discouraged, lean on the other's sense of optimism and encouragement when times are tough. If you're a laid-back person, pick up tips from your partner's sense of organization and time management. If you're overly regimented, let your spouse

"loosen" you up with his or her "go with the flow" timing over the weekend.

- Establish common team goals and share the load in reaching them (for example, financial goals, community involvement, education of the children).

- Share your fun. Fun shared tends to be twice as enjoyable.

- Cover for each other in emergencies without a sense of obligation or guilt. (If a spouse travels with the job and needs dry-cleaning done, what does it matter who takes the clothes in or picks them up? Look at each other's personal chores as team chores to be done by the person with the available time and opportunity.)

- Recognize the stress of a fast pace. Attribute petty disagreements and tensions to the true source—the pace rather than the partner.

- Communicate effectively. At the least, talking reduces tension; at best, talking resolves issues. Many couples find that they clash not about problems—in-laws, money, sex, children, groceries, carpets—but because of their communication styles. One or the other or both spouses' communication styles set them up for ongoing conflict: reacting defensively, denying, blaming, placating, dismissing, avoiding, lying, judging, issuing ultimatums, deciding without input.

Emotional support, rather than war, at home is vital to a balanced life. Expand and deepen your personal relationships to create intimacy.

TIME FOR A CHECKUP

Do you often feel and act annoyed at your spouse and children for no reason?

Do you act mentally and emotionally calm on the outside when you don't feel that way on the inside, disguising your need for connection with your family or partner?

Do you often feel like you're "walking on eggshells" when at home?

Do you lose your sense of humor and playfulness when you walk in the door at home?

Do you feel "trapped" in your marriage and with your kids?

Do you feel lonely even when your spouse and children are with you?

Do you tell your spouse or children about problems or tensions at work? Do they listen?

Do you ask your spouse or children about problems or tensions during their day? Do they seem to share them with you?

BE A REAL PARENT, NOT A SUPER PARENT

The best inheritance a parent can give his children is a few minutes of his time each day.—O. A. BATTISTA

There are only two lasting bequests we can hope to give our children. One of these is roots, the other wings.
—HODDING CARTER

If you are a happy parent, you give your son or daughter an invaluable legacy. . . . For they will grow up with the expectation that life is good, that the world is a sunny and friendly place, that other people are as human and decent as they are, that it's fun to be alive. And with that attitude they can accomplish almost anything.—GUY WRIGHT, *The San Francisco Examiner*

For some, parenting has become a job description rather than a role or relationship. You mention parenting and their mind goes to cooking, shopping, chauffeuring, sponsoring, music lessons, scouting, educational software, and SAT scores.

Yes, parenting involves all those things, but not at the same time and to the *-nth* degree. Perfect parents needle themselves with all these musts:

- I must prepare a full-course, hot breakfast for my children every morning.

- I must discuss world events with my children to help them understand the world and their place in it as they go off to school.
- I must spend time discussing "meaningful events" with my children at the end of every day.
- I must give my child opportunities to broaden cultural awareness—museums, travel, language study, art, music.
- I must oversee my child's homework projects.
- I must provide opportunity for my child to interact with those who will demand and model acceptable social stimulation.
- I must provide the latest technology to make sure my child stays ahead of the crowd and finds a rewarding career.
- I must cultivate interest in intellectual pursuits.
- I must stimulate my child's creativity.
- I must give my child all the advantages money can buy.
- I must leave my child a large inheritance.
- I must ensure that my child grows up stress-free.

In my way of thinking, parenting is more a way of loving and guiding than doing and spending. Don't let parenting become a burden rather than a joy.

Time for a Checkup

Do you look forward to being with your children every day?

Do you find yourself always nagging your children about something?

Do you force your children to go places they "should" see, investigate things they "should" learn, enjoy things they "should" benefit from?

Do you often feel guilty when you hear other parents mention activities that you have not scheduled for your children?

Are your children "scheduled" so tight that they can't be kids and let their minds roam free?

Do your children's schedules dictate your own?

Do your children's schedules and "must do's" cause conflict with your spouse?

HONOR YOUR ELDERLY PARENTS

But Be Realistic

If you don't run your own life, somebody else will.—John Atkinson

The word "altruism" offends me. Caring for others without due respect for self does not make a better world; unless we understand our own needs we cannot know the needs of others.
—Mary L. Wright

The baby-boomer generation has also been called the sandwich generation. Baby-boomers are the first group who has been crunched between the responsibility for caring (and often supporting) their adult children still living at home and their elderly parents living into their eighties and nineties.

Caring for elderly parents on a day-to-day basis can be a particularly emotionally draining experience. If the parent-child relationship has been close through the years, sometimes adult children feel guilty that they cannot give their elderly parents the constant love and attention they received growing up, and still make a living in the current hectic hubbub.

Yes, some elders may insist that you, their child, be the one to be at their side, but you, as the rational adult, know that constant care will take its toll on your own mental and emotional health. Don't push yourself to the edge of physical stamina; you'll wear yourself down mentally and emotionally, and your body will rebel under the load.

Just as you cannot shield your children from all the pain of growing up, you cannot shield your parents from all the pain of growing old. Nor will mentally healthy parents expect you to. Love and attention, yes. But *constant* care cannot be realistic for you if you have other family members depending on you for emotional energy and time.

As a caregiver, give yourself some relief from the constant demands by hiring help and by asking other family members to share the load. Just because it's your parent doesn't mean that you're the only one who must give the care. That's what marriage, family, and friendships are all about.

TIME FOR A CHECKUP

Do you feel guilty about going out for a relaxing, fun activity while leaving an elderly parent alone?

Have you actually asked others in the family to help with the care, or have you just assumed that if they wanted to help they would have volunteered?

Is care of an elderly parent creating conflict in your marriage?

ENGAGE IN MEANINGFUL CONVERSATIONS

The best of life is conversation, and the greatest success is confidence, or perfect understanding between sincere people.
—RALPH WALDO EMERSON

Conversation is an account of ourselves. . . . Conversation is the vent of character as well as of thoughts. . . . It is the laboratory of the student.—RALPH WALDO EMERSON

Education begins a gentleman. Conversation completes him.
—THOMAS FULLER

Good conversation is as stimulating as black coffee, and just as hard to sleep after.—ANNE MORROW LINDBERGH

Sweet discourse—the banquet of the mind.—JOHN DRYDEN

Do you remember those dorm parties or campfire outings when you huddled in a group and talked all night? Do you remember those heated discussions in psychology or sociology class when you exchanged answers that—had they been implemented in society—would have changed the world?

Conversation connects us with other human beings. All the meaningful relationships you have were formed by your interactions with that other person. It takes both talking and listening to make communication complete. Think what a release and relief you feel when someone truly hears you out. Consider the noble feeling of having listened well to someone and having offered them the gift of understanding.

If you want to breathe fresh air into your life, make up your mind to talk—really talk—to someone for an extended time. Call a friend for no particular reason and talk about something really important to you. Hear her or his thoughts on the subject. Listen to the friend's reactions to what you say. Brainstorm together about related solutions to any problems on your mind.

And if your friends are living at such a hectic pace that they can't find the time for such conversations, share your thoughts with an elderly family member. Or, go to a nursing home and you'll find a ready audience—and often deep wisdom. As a teenager, I often visited nursing homes as part of a service organization and can still recall the feelings stirred inside when some of the residents there gave me their undivided attention for half an hour of listening.

Engaging in a deep conversation can make you feel alive again.

Time for a Checkup

Has your talk at work become nothing more than a recital of the day's news or projects?

Has your talk at home become nothing more than an exchange of schedule information with family members?

When you go out to dinner with your teens or spouse, who generates the topics? Does your mind wander?

What is the most significant or meaningful discussion you've had in the past month? (Does nothing come to mind?)

How long has it been since someone really listened to you about a troubling situation in your life?

RESOLVE ONGOING CONFLICT WITH OTHERS

Sometimes I get the feeling that the whole world is against me, but deep down I know that's not true. Some of the smaller countries are neutral.—ROBERT ORBEN

If you're losing a tug-of-war with a tiger, give him the rope before he gets to your arm. You can always buy a new rope.
—MAX GUNTHER

Live as if you were to live forever; live as if you were to die tomorrow.—ALGERIAN PROVERB

Our bathtub had a crack in it. And the job was too small to be profitable for several marble companies we called about repair. Finally, we found someone willing to take on the job—the company bidding on the marble work in our new home under construction. They sent someone to see the crack, gave us a bid of $150, and sent a repair person (Tim) out. He didn't bring the right tools to complete the job the first time and made an appointment a few days later to return to complete the project. On the return day, I came home from work and waited. Tim didn't show. I called. We rescheduled. I came home from work again to meet the repair person. Again, Tim failed to show up.

Finally, I called the supervisor and told her about being stood up twice. She apologized and rescheduled, promising that Tim would show up the next day at twelve noon sharp.

For the fourth time, I go home from work; no repair person shows up. I call the supervisor. Our conversation goes like this:

"It's 12:15; I'm home, and Tim isn't here to complete the tub repairs."

"The appointment was supposed to be tomorrow."

"No, it was scheduled for today. I'm flying out of town tomorrow."

"You talked to me yesterday. And you said tomorrow."

"No. We set the appointment for today. But never mind about that. Tim has stood me up twice previously."

"Well, that's your problem and Tim's."

"What? Tim isn't your employee? He doesn't speak for the company?"

"Tim should have called in and asked us to schedule rather than trying to schedule on his own."

"But he didn't. And that's not my problem. That's an internal problem."

"That's *your* problem and *Tim's* problem. He should have called the dispatcher."

"That's a management problem. I don't know how Tim is supposed to schedule himself to work. I just know he told me he'd be here and he's not. I want a definite date and time that you are going to complete the project."

"Look, we're doing this as a favor to you."

"A favor? You're charging me $150."

"We're not making a profit on this—it's a favor."

"You may not be making a huge profit on this—but

you *are* handling a very profitable job on my new house under construction."

"Don't threaten me. We marble people work for the builders—not the homeowners."

"I'm not threatening you—I'm telling you that the tub job is not a favor. And I want it finished."

"I don't have time to stay on the phone with you. (*a*) You want us to be out there tomorrow at noon to finish the tub. (*b*) You don't want us out there tomorrow at noon. (*c*) Get off the phone—we don't need your business. Which will it be?"

As you can imagine, I was quite stunned at this juncture in the conversation. I had a tub repair that was half completed and had been unable to get anyone else interested in the small repair. And I had a major marble project half complete on the new house—one that would cost me even more to begin new with another marble company. They had me over a $16,000 marble barrel.

I stewed for days about letting that marble company finish the new construction project—or paying a premium to switch vendors in midstream. The inner turmoil—which lasted for at least a week in this case— came from feeling that I didn't have choices or that both choices were poor ones.

When we find ourselves in conflict with another person, we have four choices. The issue is deciding on the most expedient choice for any particular situation.

- Accommodate (give in to the other person)
- Compromise (give up some of your goals or wants)
- Overpower (insist on your way, even if angering the other person)

■ Resolve the issue (develop new alternatives so that
both of you still reach your goals and feel good about
the situation)

On occasion, any of these actions or reactions are
appropriate. What creates emotional chaos is feeling
that we have no choice in a matter. For example, if we
"give in," we may feel "taken advantage of." If we overpower, we may feel guilty. If we compromise, we regret
not getting the end result we wanted or needed.

I finally decided to settle for an apology from the
marble company sales representative and have them
finish both jobs rather than start over at a higher price.
A conscious choice to live with the decision mitigated
my anger at being treated so rudely.

Ongoing conflict—and feeling always the victim—
wears you down emotionally. I felt worn down just
recounting the conversation to the general contractor
and my family—and that was a relatively minor issue.

With more significant issues lasting over time, that
turmoil multiplies tenfold.

If you have one particular person that constantly
makes you feel drained, consider your four choices to
handle the situation involving this person. Choose the
best reaction or reactions. Then let go of the situation.
The anger or guilt sets in when you fail to recognize
that you have a choice in the matter, when you feel
that you have been forced to act or react one way or
the other. Just keep reminding yourself that you can
choose how to handle conflict. If you don't like past
choices, choose differently.

If you still cannot get past the negative feeling of
conflict, figure out a way to minimize contact with the

difficult person. If the conflict is with a family member, consider counseling from a professional.

Ongoing conflict is like a simmering pot of water. You're ready to boil over at the slightest provocation. In a bubbling state, you will never experience calmness and peace within yourself.

TIME FOR A CHECKUP

Do you dread being around a certain person, even though there's no particular issue to resolve?

Do you feel angry at yourself for "giving in" during a conflict?

Do you feel guilty for "running over" someone else just because you have the authority or position to do so?

Are you embarrassed that others know about an ongoing conflict between you and another person?

DON'T FIGHT LOST CAUSES

CHANGE YOUR MIND WHEN YOU'RE FIGHTING AN UPHILL BATTLE

It is always a great mistake to command when you are not sure you will be obeyed.—HONORÉ GABRIEL MIRABEAU

Ride the horse in the direction that it's going.—WERNER ERHARD

What we believe we can control, we often can't. And what we believe we cannot control, we often can. Power comes in knowing the difference.

At one time in my life, I was locked into a relationship in which the other person suffered (and I do mean suffered) from poor self-esteem. As a result, he lived his life as self-fulfilling prophecy, with a defeatist attitude. He couldn't get to work on time, he couldn't get along with bosses, he couldn't learn a new job, he couldn't make "the right" decision.

Erroneously, I thought I could change things for him by offering enough acceptance and encouragement. But no amount of determination on *my* part could change his own opinion of himself. It took me a long time to learn that I couldn't improve things for him—that I had absolutely no control in the situation. When I stopped butting my head against that wall, life sure felt a lot better.

Some people fight losing battles all day: They don't like company policies and continue to resent and resist them. They don't like bosses and continue to berate and sabotage them. They don't like the neighborhood, but can't afford to move. They don't like the way their social club or professional organization is run, but they continue to attend and complain.

Other examples? Changing an elderly parent's disposition. Motivating an adult son or daughter to take responsibility for his or her life. Changing the investment objectives of your firm. Changing the culture of an entire organization singlehandedly. Determining a friend's moral values.

Sometimes people spend time wrestling with matters that are trivial in the big scheme of things. They resist change simply because it's change. Sooner or later, most people come to realize that they can't wage a war on all fronts at once. They have to prioritize their battles, grumblings, and enemies.

Resistance to ideas and change drains energy. Decide what you can and cannot change or control in your life. Make room in your attitude to accommodate the difference.

Time for a Checkup

How many minutes do you spend each week complaining about company policies or procedures you can't change?

How many hours a year do you spend fighting irreversible community decisions?

How many significant "battles" has your resistance won in the last ten years?

Have other people in the same circumstances as you seemingly adjusted and "gone on" with their lives?

SETTLE THINGS

Don't Let Disappointment Disorient You

The reason for most folks' dissatisfaction in life is that they are looking for a custom fit in an off-the-rack world.
—GARY GULBRANSON

All men should strive to learn before they die what they are running from, and to, and why.—JAMES THURBER

For everything you have missed you have gained something.
—RALPH WALDO EMERSON

We do not do what we want, and yet we are responsible for what we are.—JEAN-PAUL SARTRE

Sometimes people who are the most productive, most creative, most responsible, and most caring feel more disappointment in life than others. Because they have a higher standard and a higher sensitivity than others, they feel more deeply disappointed with the way things are.

For example, leaders feel a conflict with what they would like to achieve in their community or organization and what they can realistically achieve. Writers experience the conflict with their drive to create The Great American Novel, yet face the reality of how few manuscripts get published. Soldiers have concern about their comrades falling around them, yet feel driven to push ahead against the enemy to save other lives depending on them. Artists experience the urge to create beauty while struggling with the need to make a living.

And then there are the lesser issues of life. The day-to-day stuff we can't seem to settle and put aside. Like hating in-laws because of the way they reared your spouse. Like being overweight and wanting to be a thin waif. Like blaming another race or individual for your own economic condition. Like earning a living as a dentist while suppressing the dream to travel the country doing night-club acts. Like having a parent who didn't love you. Like having a lousy first marriage. Like raising ungrateful, selfish kids. Like having a bad knee that kept you from getting a baseball scholarship. Like not being able to graduate from an Ivy League school.

We've labeled many irrational jumps in mood or disruptions of families as midlife crises. But more likely, that conflict has been smoldering under the surface of consciousness for an extended time before midlife.

Some people keep grappling with the same life issues month after month, year after year. They lapse into guilt, self-pity, anger, or depression. Any of or all these can be excuses for not accepting life and change and moving on into the future.

Disappointment and turmoil create stress. Be resilient. March on.

TIME FOR A CHECKUP

List all the major things you've been disappointed about. How many of those things have you "stewed over" for more than a year? More than five years? More than fifteen years?

What goals have you not accomplished because of your feelings about these issues?

Who or what are you blaming for failure to live the lifestyle of your choice?

MELT ANGER TO RELEASE EXTRA ENERGY

Anger is often more hurtful than the injury that caused it.
—PROVERB

There isn't enough time for love, so what does that leave for hate?—BILL COPELAND, THE SARASOTA JOURNAL

The best cure for the body is to quiet the mind.—NAPOLEON

For every minute you are angry, you lose 60 seconds of happiness.—RALPH WALDO EMERSON

On a recent trip to Bangkok, my husband and I visited a local tailor to have a few suits made. Our agreement was that we would have two fittings and that the clothes would be finished in time for us to check fit and quality before we left the country on the following Wednesday.

Here's the typical scenario for tailors dealing with tourists: When a customer walks through the door, the tailor finds out their departure flight, and then works backward to juggle jobs to meet various departure dates. The long and short of our story in Bangkok was that we contacted the tailor in plenty of time to have our clothes finished, but the tailor kept "working other customers in" so that our clothes were not delivered to the hotel until an hour before flight time. They didn't fit. We refused to take them. The tailor argued about refunding the upfront payment.

The entire last day of the trip was ruined because I kept reliving the scene—kept arguing with the tailor who had promised the two fittings that didn't materialize and who didn't deliver the clothes to fit and on time. When the courier delivered the clothes to the hotel lobby as we were departing the city, I had to go through the entire agreement with him. Then again with the salesperson, who suddenly arrived on the scene. Then again with the sales manager, who was determined that either I or his salesperson would pay for the foul-up. Then I relived the scene each time I told someone back home about it the day we returned to work. And again two days later when I wrote the credit card company about subtracting the payment from my bill.

I needed another day of vacation to recover from the energy spent on the turmoil.

If you spend a lot of time in an angry or tense state of mind, stress-related hormones are discharged into the body. This discharge triggers the production of blood fats that cling to the artery walls, thus reducing the amount of oxygen going to the heart. Stress also raises your blood pressure If you relive an incident of anger over and over, your nervous system stays on red alert. The effects are toxic to your system.

And as your stress increases with the resulting bodily reactions, your energy wanes. If you want to increase your energy, decrease your anger. Learn to let go of things.

TIME FOR A CHECKUP

sDo people frequently, for no apparent reason, ask you, "What's wrong?"

Is your natural, typical facial expression a frown or scowl?

Do you still get visibly angry (red-faced, emotional, high-pitched voice) when you recall something that happened yesterday? A week ago? A month ago?

Do you transfer anger—become irritable with those who happen to be around you rather than with those who caused a bad situation?

DOODLE IN A
DIARY ABOUT
YOUR
EMOTIONAL
JOURNEY

Life is a process of burning oneself out and time is the fire that burns you. —TENNESSEE WILLIAMS

Do you ever feel like you're reasoning in circles, that you keep doing 180-degree turns in making decisions?

In my own life, I've used writing in a diary as a way to keep score, to review where I've been in struggling with a decision, and to remind myself about redundant thinking and loops along the way. Then from time to time when puzzled about the same issue, I can reread my thinking to see if I'm at least charting new emotional waters.

Write only when you feel like it and have the time. Many people find writing a way to release stress or anger and to come to conclusions and wisdom.

Psychologists often recommend to patients that they write a letter to air their grievances and release the anger. Whether they mail the letter is irrelevant to the effect it has on the psyche.

Writing things down clarifies feelings, assumptions, and conclusions. The time between rereadings provides perspective.

Time for a Checkup

Reread an old love letter you've written someone. Do you have a different perspective or feelings at this point in your life?

Do you feel better after writing a complaint letter to a store manager after bad service?

PLAN WORRY TIME

The big, tough, important things I can get through . . . but then I walk out of the house and into the clothesline.—WILL ROGERS

I've suffered a great many catastrophes in my life. Most of them never happened.—MARK TWAIN

Things are in the saddle and ride mankind.
—RALPH WALDO EMERSON

When you catch your mind wandering into worry, postpone the thoughts until later. (Telling yourself not to worry altogether doesn't work.) Schedule yourself a time to think about that worry; jot it down if you must. (My worry notes are usually titled, "What to do about . . .") Then tell yourself you've got to focus on the task at hand and that you'll focus on the worry at the scheduled time.

At the scheduled time, focus on your worries. First, sort your worries into those that are real and those that may never happen. For those that may never happen, promise to worry about them when and if they happen. To lessen the anxiety during the waiting time, use the old principle: "What's the worst thing that can happen to me? Will I survive?" "If I'll survive, under what conditions will I be forced to live?" "If I'm forced to live under those conditions, how will I cope?" Work backward to lessen the anxiety.

For example, here's one of my worries that never happened: Several years ago a publisher called me to say they had gone to press with my book. Shocked at their being ahead of schedule, I asked her to fax the jacket copy, which they'd somehow forgotten to let me proof. I panicked. It seems they had decided to use the name of one of my largest clients in big bold letters as part of the copy. Without asking me. What kind of clearance did we need? Was this a legal issue? What if the client objected? What if the client decided to cancel the $70,000 worth of training workshops for the coming year? What if the client decided never to do business with me again? What if the client sued us and put us out of business?

I lay awake for three nights. Then the worry settled into a big dread about publication day three months away—the day the book was to appear in the bookstores and my client would discover its name on the jacket. Finally, the publisher's release date came and went. Fearing the worst, I mailed a copy to my client contact and braced for the fallout. Another two weeks passed before he called to say, "Well, looks like we finally made the cover of one of your books! We're impressed!" End of discussion. Three months of sleepless nights over a worry that never happened.

I made a pact with myself after that incident. There are too many potential worries in running a business. I can afford the time and energy only on the real worries that happen.

For the real worries that deserve attention, focus on them at the scheduled time. Take the worry apart and try to outline steps you can take to prevent the situation, correct the problem, or minimize the impact. Then take action toward a resolution.

Your action may not improve the situation, but you'll feel less anxiety about doing than worrying.

TIME FOR A CHECKUP

List your worries for the last year. Which have really happened?

Of the worries that have really happened, which could you have prevented with more worry and attention?

ENGAGE IN SELF-TALK THAT UPLIFTS

Man is not the creature of circumstances. Circumstances are the creatures of men.—BENJAMIN DISRAELI

People will be just about as happy as they will allow themselves to be.—ABRAHAM LINCOLN

The list of negative self-talk can be endless:

- There is a right way and wrong way to do something. I always do it wrong." (*Positive:* There's more than one way to do anything.)

- "Mistakes are irreversible and damaging." (*Positive:* Mistakes happen. They're the price of eventual success.)

- "People may not like me, and that would be too painful to chance." (*Positive:* I have my friends. I can stand it if someone is displeased with me.)

- "People may criticize me and think I am bad or wrong." (*Positive:* People will always criticize. I can take my share.)

- "Life should be fair." (*Positive:* I roll with the punches.)

- "Other people get away with things that I don't." (*Positive:* I'm often lucky and get away with things when others don't.)

- "Other people don't have the hardships that I have." (*Positive:* Handling hardships has made me a stronger person.)

- "I must have a best friend with me all the time." (*Positive:* I enjoy my own company. I'm happy to be alone at times.)

- "I get stuck with all the projects nobody else wants to do." (*Positive:* They know I'll always come through. They need me.)

- "Other people enjoy their work more than I enjoy mine." (*Positive:* Everybody occasionally does drudge work, me included.)

- "Other people have loving families, and I don't." (*Positive:* I'm like many people who don't have family relationships.)

- "Everybody but me enjoys wonderful vacations." (*Positive:* I'm like many people who occasionally take simple, quiet vacations.)

- "I deserve happiness all the time—why don't I feel happy?" (*Positive:* I can be as happy as I make up my mind to be.)

- "People break promises to me all the time. I'm a wimp." (*Positive:* I can stand up to people if I choose to be assertive.)

- "Technology will ruin my life. I can't learn to deal with it." (*Positive:* Technology can improve my life. I can choose to deal with it.)

- "I'll never have enough money to feel secure, so I can never relax and spend for 'extras.'" (*Positive:* I can manage my money so that I feel secure in knowing what's available for "extras.")

- "Other people manage their money better than I do." (*Positive:* I can learn to manage my money better.)
- "I never get lucky breaks like other people." (*Positive:* Sometimes I'm lucky. I can manage my "breaks" like other people.)
- "I'm just not as smart as most people." (*Positive:* I'm a capable person.)
- "I must anticipate what tomorrow will bring, and stay one step ahead." (*Positive:* No one knows the future, but whatever happens, I'll manage it.)
- "I will always feel behind in my work." (*Positive:* My work will always feel challenging to me. I can change jobs if I choose to do so.)
- "I will never achieve my most important goals." (*Positive:* I can set and achieve important goals.)
- "It is too late for me to change." (*Positive:* It's never too late to change.)
- "I cannot afford to take a risk because if I fail I'll be worse off than before." (*Positive:* Taking risks makes life exciting and satisfying. If I fail, I can go on.)

If you have difficulty talking to yourself with praise rather than condemnation, try this project: Collect all your commendation letters, notes, certificates, and medals you've received through the years and put them out as visual reminders of your successes. Some people call this their "I love me" drawer or wall or room.

For another step in the right direction, when people compliment you, listen and enjoy their comments. When you notice that you've done something well, give yourself approval and a reward (time off, time spent in fun activity, a dessert).

Negative self-talk creates depression and stress. Challenge unfounded assumptions and conclusions. Praise yourself. Talk to yourself rationally. Promise yourself a bright future.

TIME FOR A CHECKUP

Do you feel "down" for no apparent reason?

Have you congratulated yourself for not having declared bankruptcy at this point in your life?

Have you congratulated yourself for having people who love you?

Have you celebrated your ability to hold a responsible position or job?

Do you give yourself credit for living independently and being capable of making your own decisions?

Have you realized how smart you must be to buy self-help books and learn from other people's experiences?

LEARN WHAT LEISURE IS

There is no pleasure in having nothing to do; the fun is in having lots to do and not doing it.—JOHN W. RAPER

We do not stop playing because we are old, we grow old because we stop playing.—ANONYMOUS

In every real man a child is hidden that wants to play.
—FRIEDRICH NIETZSCHE

In his thought-provoking book *Living Without Goals*, James Ogilvy analyzes the life of billionaire recluse Howard Hughes: "His life was exemplary in ways that make him worth monitoring as an early warning system for the rest of us in our pursuit of Goals, which if we could see them more clearly realized, we might not want. He achieved the Goals of wealth and fame and power but died a hermit's death." Yes, Hughes inherited a fortune from his father, who had founded Hughes Tool Company. He also founded and built TWA airlines. In his spare time, he earned the reputation as a Hollywood tycoon, a movie producer, and a celebrity maker. He worshiped beautiful women and money. In the process of living, he became fabulously wealthy but lost his ability to enjoy his winnings.

Leisure can never be an end in itself. It needs a purpose. That purpose can be relaxation and refreshment of the mind.

Remember the warnings about the impending four-day work week, warnings that we'd better be prepared for a generation of leisure? In the 1990s, most of have gone too far in the opposite direction. Rather than pursuing a life of pleasure, we have forgotten what leisure feels like.

Ask people at a cocktail party what they do for leisure, and they'll probably answer, "What's leisure?" In our penchant for productivity in the last decade, some work cultures have stigmatized leisure. Nobody wants to admit that they need, want, or enjoy leisure. If you're one of these people, get over it.

Leisure can serve as a short purpose on our longer journey to *a purpose*. It's okay to admit that you might have time for leisure. Let me define leisure with a few specifics:

- Read cartoons, comics, entertaining columns, poems, or articles on topics that interests you (not work-related).
- Relax with a favorite food or beverage.
- Browse in a toy or gadget store.
- Browse in a card shop and read all the funny and sentimental cards.
- Browse in an antique mall for collectibles.
- Go to a movie on Tuesday night.
- Pop popcorn and watch a video on Thursday afternoon.
- Watch a sports event.
- Play a sport.
- Visit an amusement park.

- Sit outside on the patio and watch the neighborhood kids play.
- Go for a leisurely walk—not an exercise walk.
- Invite someone to meet you somewhere in the middle of the day for brunch or late lunch.
- Stroll through model homes.
- Enjoy a hobby.
- Dance.
- Go sightseeing in your own city.
- Work a puzzle.
- Watch wildlife.
- Take photographs.
- Look at old photographs.
- Try new recipes and invite a favorite person to sample them.
- Have a party—theme, decorations, games, the works.
- Play with electronic gadgets.
- Surf the Internet.

How do you manage time for leisure? Can you do something during your commute to work? Take a half-hour break during the work day? Leave work early once a month? Stay up an extra hour one night a week? Get up an hour earlier on Saturday? Amuse yourself while waiting for an appointment? Amuse yourself while standing in a waiting line? Do your work in a fun setting?

Leisure time well spent increases your energy, improves your concentration, refreshes your attitude, and makes you more productive when you return to work.

Time for a Checkup

Are you embarrassed to say that you have leisure time?

What activities have you done in the last month— just for the fun of them?

Do you use your leisure time as a refreshing time or do you just "kill time"?

Do you have to work at having fun?

Do you catch yourself sitting at your desk but unable to concentrate on the work at hand?

If so, do you take a break for leisure or just force yourself to sit and "try"?

REST AND SLEEP MORE

Fatigue makes cowards of us all.—VINCE LOMBARDI

The time to relax is when you don't have time for it.
—SYDNEY J. HARRIS

According to neuroscientists, sleep is critical for key brain functions: learning, performance, memory. A 1995 survey by the Better Sleep Council (reported in *Training* magazine, July 1995) revealed that 53 percent of respondents acknowledged that their mental capabilities suffered when they lost sleep. One-third of the respondents reported that they didn't get enough sleep.

Forty percent of the respondents reported that stress keeps them awake at night. Clearly, handling stress better allows you to fall asleep more quickly and stay asleep throughout the night. You can work to improve most other skills. But as with sex and sleep, you can't force yourself to perform or enjoy.

What you *can* do is allow yourself more time to sleep. My husband can decide to go to bed at 8 p.m. one night a week and catch up. He can fall asleep within minutes. For other people, the once-a-week or once-a-month effort doesn't work; they have to establish a routine bedtime. If that's the case for you, gradually work your bedtime forward in five-minute increments until you are getting an extra half hour of sleep each night.

Or, you might try a sleep marathon occasionally. Plan ahead for uninterrupted sleep and sleep as long as you can without becoming bored in bed.

You'll enjoy it. You'll feel refreshed. Your brain will function better.

Likewise, schedule yourself a day of rest each week. A day when you can mentally unwind from work-related responsibilities. A pastor friend of mine used to quip, "You can follow God's commandment to rest one day a week, or you can take your rest days all in a row—in the hospital."

TIME FOR A CHECKUP

Do you feel refreshed when you wake up in the mornings?

Do you rest your mind by doing things unrelated to your work at least one day a week?

EXERCISE—PLAY LIKE RECESS

Activity strengthens. Inactivity weakens.—Hippocrates

Those who do not find time for exercise will have to find time for illness.—Proverb

Health is the thing that makes you feel now is the best time of the year.—Franklin P. Adams

A man is as old as his arteries.—Thomas Sydenham

Exercise and health are closely related to time. We have less time to stay healthy. Some people live as if it's easier to get their bodies fixed after they rebel than to eat right or exercise regularly. For some, it's more convenient to be off work for two months with a heart attack than to take half an hour every day to exercise to prevent one.

Bodies have memories. They bear the scars of neglect. If you treat your body right, it will serve you a long time. If you treat it poorly, it will play out on you quickly.

Exercise does two things for you: It improves your physical health, and it relieves your stress.

Do you remember how good it felt back in elementary school when you got to go outside at recess and run and play? Hard play. Running around the bases. Playing Red Rover, Red Rover. Playing chase. Pumping yourself or a friend on the swings. When you returned to the classroom, you could do your multiplication tables much faster.

Exercise for the fun of it, not for the work of it. Don't make it another item on your to-do list by participating in something rigid—like having to go to the gym to use the equipment there or having to make your aerobic class at 6:00 on Tuesday and Thursday evenings.

Instead, choose something that requires no equipment, no special clothing, no certain time, no certain location. Isometrics, aerobic movements, walking. Or any variation thereof. As a traveler, I've discovered many playful recesses that fit the single criteria of exercise: walking up and down flights of stairs, walking down long hotel hallways, jogging or walking in place in my hotel room, doing aerobic movements while watching the TV or listening to the radio.

To restore your inner calmness and refresh your spirit, play hard—like recess.

Time for a Checkup

Do you consider exercise an obligation that you schedule?

Do you look forward to letting your mind wander free during periods of exercise?

Do you exercise hard enough to "work up a sweat"?

Have you considered having a friend or family member join you to exercise?

EAT TO STAY HEALTHY

People believe in better living through chemistry. They would rather take a pill than stay away from cheeseburgers and shakes.—JERRY AVON, MD

I saw few die of hunger, of eating, 100,000.
—BENJAMIN FRANKLIN

Your body is the baggage you must carry through life. The more excess baggage the shorter the trip.—ARNOLD H. GLASGOW

Whichever your philosophy—eating to live or living to eat—mealtime doesn't have to be a time-consuming ordeal. With Americans' penchant for grabbing junk food on the run, combined with media attention on fitness and nutrition, food companies are now trying to accommodate both trends: fast and healthy.

You no longer have to shop, thaw, marinate, simmer, and scrub to eat right. Fast food can be healthy food. My typical routine is cold cereal or a bagel for breakfast, yogurt and fruit for lunch, and vegetables or a baked potato for dinner. My husband wants something more substantial, so he opts for fish and chicken at lunch or dinner. And the larger food companies even offer ready-to-bake entrees to meet a hearty appetite. More and more delis also cater to the family who wants to pick up a bowl of baked beans and pasta salad on the way home from work.

Being a frequent traveler, I've also noticed that more and more restaurants have menus to accommodate healthy and fast. Forget the menus—just ask for what you want, and they'll bring it out and give you a price on the spot. Often I leave a hotel in the morning before the coffee shop opens, so I call the kitchen the night before and ask for a couple of pieces of fruit to be sent to my room. (It may or may not be sent on time, but poor customer service is another story....)

Kids need guidance about nutrition as well. They like what they learn to like. If they begin life eating healthy food, they typically cultivate and maintain that taste and inclination toward nutritious foods. Is it possible to raise children without candy, chips, pretzels, and sugar-coated cereal in the house? Yes.

Fast and healthy are no longer mutually exclusive. Mealtime doesn't have to be a major production.

TIME FOR A CHECKUP

Would you like to lose weight?

Do you have health problems that can be traced to poor eating habits?

Do you know the location of delis and food stores that cater to the health-conscious shopper?

LAUGH MORE AND MORE OFTEN

A merry heart does good like a medicine.—PROVERBS 17:22

When my son Jeff was about 4 years old, we took him to the Denver zoo. His favorite attraction happened to be the monkeys. Just as we stopped in front of the cage, the monkeys decided to put on a real show, jumping from limb to limb, making faces, slapping each other upside the head. Watching them, Jeff began to giggle. Then he began to laugh from the belly. Then he began to laugh hysterically. Before we knew it, a crowd of passersby had gathered around to watch him laugh. Then *they all* began to laugh at his laughing and amusement over the monkeys. Even now every time I recall the scene, I can almost hear the delighted giggling.

Laughter is contagious.

As Norman Cousins noted in his book *Anatomy of an Illness,* laughter also contributes to wellness. When Mr. Cousins discovered he had a rare disease and became bedfast, he set about to cure himself with laughter. The book is his account of his successful efforts to laugh himself back to health. Laughter causes the brain to create endorphins that reduce stress. Although doctors don't understand all the whys and hows, these joy-induced endorphins also improve the immune system's ability to fight off disease.

When life gets so hectic that you can't remember when you last smiled, you need a good belly-laugh. Look for the humor in everyday situations. A laugh a day, as well as the proverbial apple, may keep the doctor away.

TIME FOR A CHECKUP

Do you read the comics routinely?

Have you videotaped comedy routines for "reruns" at your convenience?

Do you habitually restrain laughter when someone attempts a witty remark or funny story?

When's the last time you told someone "a funny thing happened on the way to work" story?

ENJOY SEX
MORE OFTEN

You can't eat for eight hours a day nor drink for eight hours a day nor make love for eight hours a day—all you can do for eight hours is work. Which is the reason why man makes himself and everybody else so miserable and unhappy.
—WILLIAM FAULKNER

Love affairs nowadays often proceed without the frills of those in past decades. No lengthy courtships. No time wasted in planning "chance" meetings with only opportunities for glances across the room. No time wasted in elaborate conversations to learn about one's past or one's future plans. No time to meet the family.

Even sex is a by-product of time. According to the latest sex surveys by Masters and Johnson, rather than the earlier-reported twice-a-week sexual activity, the average couple now says their hectic pace of life has reduced their lovemaking to once a week. We've been aware of the connection between time and sex every since statisticians began reporting the rise in birth rates nine months after big snowstorms or blackouts. Likewise, in underdeveloped countries, birth rates go down when installation of electricity goes up.

My hunch is that alternative activities do not do nearly as much good for the psyche as intimacy with the one we love.

TIME FOR A CHECKUP

During times of stress, do you make love more or less often?

When is the last time you planned lovemaking for a time other than at night when you and your loved one were exhausted?

TAKE REAL, RESTFUL VACATIONS AND MINI-VACATIONS

Last year we discovered a vacation spot that's convenient to get to, comfortable, relaxing, where we don't have to get dressed up, and that's priced within our budget. It's called the living room.—ROBERT ORBEN

The end of labor is to gain leisure.—ARISTOTLE

A vacation is like a romance: anticipated with pleasure; experienced with discomfort; remembered with nostalgia.
—LOU ERICKSON

"Productive Vacations." This oxymoron appeared as a headline in a recent issue of *Success* magazine. The article went on to report that vacations are no longer fun and games. According to a study by Steelcase, Inc. and Bruskin Goldring Research, 23 percent of Americans are taking their work to the beach, to the mountains, to the resort to work during vacation. George Bell of Steelcase was quoted as saying, "The added flexibility gives people more choices about when and where they work, allowing them to better balance their work and personal life."

I question whether this is the most appropriate use of freedom our technology has provided.

One of the best policies that corporate America has clung to is this one regarding vacation days: Use them or lose them. Corporations grant so many paid vacation days each year and expect you to use them, because conventional wisdom says mental recesses and "downtime" refreshen our perspective and increase productivity.

If you're one of the more than 9 million self-employed Americans and don't have staff to "cover" for you, technology that travels with you may allow you at least a change of scenery while you "stay in touch." But then I wouldn't call the time away a real vacation.

If the nature of your job is such that you can't take a full week or two of vacation, consider mini-vacations of two or three days over a long weekend—time that you can really call your own without having to touch a keyboard or keypad.

Also consider the kind of vacation you need. There are two kinds of vacationers in the world: those who use vacations as a chance to travel, sightsee, learn and those who expect to sleep until noon and do nothing the rest of the time. Unfortunately, in many situations, these two kinds of vacationers are married to each other. If that's the case, you may have to make a trade-off and alternate vacation types from year to year.

Because last year's schedule was the most hectic I've had in a while, my husband and I opted for a four-day mini-vacation of do-nothing. After I finished a speech in British Columbia last December, we checked into a deserted mountain resort and did nothing more taxing than bundle up and go for a walk through the snow at midday. We ate, slept, read, watched video movies, and then ate, slept, and read some more. We both agreed that it was the most relaxing, best vacation we've spent together.

However, if you feel the stress of a monotonous, routine job, you may enjoy vacations with lots of fast-paced activity. Determine what you need from a vacation and plan accordingly.

TIME FOR A CHECKUP

What is your idea of a refreshing vacation—travel, sightseeing, fun and games, or rest with no schedule to meet? When's the last time you've taken such a vacation?

Do you return to work after a vacation feeling tired, or feeling rested and upbeat, with a new and improved perspective for the tasks at hand?

Considering the holiday schedule posted by your employer, how many mini-vacations (long weekends) could you plan for the year if you "spent" a few of your vacation days throughout the calendar year rather than all at once?

TAKE SHORT SABBATICALS FROM WORK AND FAMILY

There is not music in a "rest" but there's the making of music in it. And people are always missing that part of the life melody.
—JOHN RUSKIN

Take rest; a field that has rested gives a bountiful crop.—OVID

When you begin to feel like the old song, "Stop the world, I want to get off," you know you need more than a brief vacation. When dealing with true burnout, try to find other options to give yourself a few weeks or a few months to recover and regain your perspective on life.

Most true sabbaticals—situations where an employer actually pays you to take time away from your routine job to study, research, or rest—are the perks of high-ranking executives and well-tenured professors. Most companies cannot afford to let a job go undone for a long period of time. Therefore, if you're dealing with burnout and need a time-out, you'll have to construct your own. You may be able to take a leave of absence from your job, without pay, if you have trained others to take on your job responsibilities.

Here are some other possibilities: Take extra time

between a change of employers. Find a seasonal job, with built-in downtime for all employees. Become self-employed so that you have control over your hours. Redistribute or reassign your job responsibilities to others for a short period. Cut back to part-time hours for a six-month period. Set up a job-sharing situation with another burned-out coworker.

If you need a sabbatical from an exhausting or stressful family situations (such as a seriously ill family member for whose care you have primary responsibility), try reassigning a few duties to various other family members for a short period. Or, try hiring a college student or elderly worker for some of the tasks. Or, arrange to swap child care with a friend for a week. If you can't find someone else to take the heavy responsibilities of medical care, can you hire help for the less vital tasks—or let the routine tasks go undone for a few days or weeks?

Sabbaticals, whether formal or informal, may save your sanity.

Time for a Checkup

Do you feel exhausted even after the weekend and dread "another week"?

Are you willing to trade money for time off?

Are you willing to be passed over for promotion in exchange for periods of pure leisure and pursuit of different goals?

PLAN FOR YOUR WEEKENDS

To be able to fill leisure intelligently is the last product of civilization.—BERTRAND RUSSELL

If you want something to happen, make a space for it.
—DAVID CAMPBELL

When my husband and I started dating, we planned every weekend starting on Monday. We shopped antique malls. We entered 10K runs. We scouted out renaissance festivals, rodeos, museums. We landscaped. We attended the kids' school or church events. We hosted parties. Then we had all week to discuss the details and look forward to the relaxing, change-of-pace fun at the end of the labor.

But then somewhere between our third and fourth years of marriage, we discovered that our weekends had become "catch-up" duties of the previous week or "get-ahead" projects to carry us through the following week. With nothing special to look forward to, the weekends generated about as much enthusiasm as Monday morning did. Consequently, we've returned to the habit of planning our weekends to make them special.

Of course, you can't always take the entire weekend to live it as you'd like, but you can plan a few events to make it fun and different from the remainder of your week. The difference in mindset and enthusiasm creates balance.

TIME FOR A CHECKUP

Have your weekend activities for the last month generated any story worth telling at work on Monday morning?

Have you eaten at a nice (not fast-food) restaurant in the last month?

Have you done anything that required advance tickets in the last month?

Have you done anything that required a babysitter in the last month?

If you were dating—rather than married to—your mate, would you have made different plans for this past weekend?

COCOON TILL
YOU GO CRAZY

The last and greatest art is to limit and isolate oneself.
—Johann Wolfgang von Goethe

You've got to decide on an inner discipline to protect yourself. Step out of the interesting dynamic rhythm every so often and focus on your internal life.—Naomi Rosenblatt

Your idea of bliss is to wake up on a Monday morning knowing you haven't a single engagement for the entire week. You are cradled in a white paper cocoon tied up with typewriter ribbon.—Edna Ferber, On Uninterrupted Writing

When we moved into our new community, the neighbors commented on our "fast-paced" lifestyle—when all they knew about our schedule was the coming and going from our garage. In most mindsets, activity—fast or slow—translates to hectic.

When you're riding a train, the sensation of speed comes from the scenery you see speeding by the window. The same can be true of life. The sensation of the hectic pace is often generated by the frequency of dressing and undressing to go somewhere. Of deciding to do or not to do something. Of mingling with groups of people after groups of people.

To get a sense of slowing down your life, try cocooning for short periods of time. The term first came into our vocabulary with the advent of technology that permitted us to access all the services like shopping, banking, communicating via the computer without ever having to leave home.

Although I don't choose to handle all my business this way, I do suggest the change of pace of staying at home for an extended period of time. Generally, when my husband is away on business, I take that opportunity to cocoon for a week at a time. I don't put on makeup. I don't dress up. I don't go out to the grocery store. I don't phone my friends or family to chat. I don't drive anywhere. Then I replace all the don't-want-to-do's with what I *want* to do—from home.

Cocooning provides opportunity to live life "off stage." Mental downtime. Physical downtime. Emotional downtime. A by-product is more productive time to do what you enjoy.

TIME FOR A CHECKUP

Do you live in your house or just exist there on your way someplace else?

How many times a week do you enter and leave your house?

How many minutes a week could you save by "doing errands" from home—by phone, by mail, by computer—or by postponing them until you are going to be out anyway?

REENERGIZE
WITH RITUALS

Enthusiasm and persistence can make an average person superior; indifference and lethargy can make a superior person average.—William A. Ward

If people are going to be peak performers, they have to know how to change their energy state.—Ken Blanchard

We act as though comfort and luxury were the chief requirements of life, when all we need to make us really happy is something to be enthusiastic about.—Charles Kingsley

Energy enthusiast Dr. Ann Cooper-McGee suggests an approach called "energy engineering," which involves making a list of things that give you energy and things that drain your energy. My list includes the following:

What Gives Me Energy	What Drains My Energy
Walking in the woods	Waiting in service or checkout lines
Having someone ask my advice on a troubling issue	Boring speakers
Country-western music	Following up on a myriad of small details
Compliments about my books	Fear of confrontations
Selecting decorator knickknacks for the house	Traffic

WHAT GIVES ME ENERGY	WHAT DRAINS MY ENERGY
Discussing the dialogue or characterization in a movie I've just seen	Meeting constant deadlines
Attending worship services	
Speaking to an eager audience	Vacuuming
Visiting people in a different culture or circumstance	Running errands
Reading funny verses in greeting cards	

Observe your own moods and energy levels, and make your own list. Then plan how you can structure more energy-inducing items, activities, or images into your day-to-day life.

For my husband, watching a good western on TV adds that sense of renewal. Speaker friends of mine report rituals such as taking audiotapes of favorite music, scented candles, and nail-care items to treat themselves to a luxurious bath-and-beauty ritual upon checking into a strange hotel in a strange city to address a strange audience.

One family in Boulder, Colorado, enjoys a pajama party on Saturday nights. Everyone changes into pajamas so they can do the family wash, and they make homemade pizza together as they fold clothes, iron, and put away the laundry.

Most families have holiday rituals; they add nostalgia and sentiment to the occasion. But why wait for the holidays? Make opportunities to spread rituals throughout your year and during your days.

TIME FOR A CHECKUP

What is a relaxing Saturday morning ritual for you? What relaxing week-night ritual would improve your outlook the next morning at work?

READ TO REGAIN YOUR PERSPECTIVE

A man who wants time to read and write lets the grass grow long.—SLOAN WILSON

Everyman is the creature of the age in which he lives; very few are able to raise themselves above the ideas of the times.
—VOLTAIRE

Nothing can transport me from the day-to-day to the sublime like a good novel or a thought-provoking essay. When you feel as though the world is coming unglued, regain your footing by examining a deep thought some writer has set forth. For just such occasions, I keep a reading *pile*—quite different from my reading *file*. The reading file contains magazines, journals, and newsletters that provide information on industry trends and professional how-tos. But when I need to relax, I go to my pile of recently purchased books or old ones on the shelf.

Reading provides new insights, emotional thrills, and vicarious experiences without your ever having to leave your chair. If your own life seems unbalanced, reading reconfirms that there's more to the world than you're experiencing at the moment. That thought often keeps present trouble in perspective.

TIME FOR A CHECKUP

How long has it been since you've read a good novel?

How long has it been since you've read a good nonfiction book outside your work interest?

How long has it been since you've read an essay in a magazine or newspaper that caused you to think deeply about something outside your own daily experiences?

How long since you've read something by E. B. White, Mark Twain, Will Rogers, William Faulkner, Eudora Welty, Maya Angelou, Beverly Lowery, e e cummings, Ernest Hemingway, Erma Bombeck, C. S. Lewis?

REENERGIZE YOURSELF WITH DREAMS AND VISUALIZATIONS

We need time to dream, time to remember, and time to reach the infinite. Time to be.—GLADYS TABER

When you let your dreams die, something dies within you.
—DENSON FRANKLIN

"I'd like to drive all through the backroads from state to state and visit all the county courthouses."

"I'd like to have my dad come for a visit so we could do a wood-working project together—like build a swing set for the backyard."

"I'd like to live right on the lake so I could walk out in the backyard and drop my fishing line in the water without having to get out in the boat."

"I'd like to coauthor a book with you on the sense of brotherhood and sacrifice during war."

All these statements are dreams expressed by my husband at one time or another. And each time he speaks of one of these wishes, his face lights up, his voice grows animated, and his mind whirrs.

The first few times he expressed these dreams of the future, I took it upon myself to react with reality:

When? Where? How could we do that? My penchant for reality put a kink in the whole scene.

I've since learned the importance of dreams—not to do, but to dare.

TIME FOR A CHECKUP

Do you have a dream that generates enthusiasm whenever you think of it?—Building a new house? Moving to the country? Selling a screenplay? Earning your doctorate?

Do you permit others close to you to reenergize themselves with dreams without trying to force them to make commitments of time or effort to accomplish that dream?

REALLY LISTEN TO MUSIC

The simplest way of listening to music is to listen for the sheer pleasure of the musical sound itself.—Aaron Copland

The habit of listening to music and of dreaming about it predisposes one to love.—Stendhal (Marie Henry Beyle)

A painter paints his pictures on canvas. But musicians paint their pictures on silence. We provide the music and you provide the silence.—Leopold Stokowski

Music plays in the elevator, in the restaurant, in the hotel lobby, in the department store, from your car radio, during TV jingles, as you "hold" on the phone, from your computer. None of that counts. Such music has just become one more sound in the cacaphonic background.

If you want a mood lift and renewed energy, listen to music *intentionally*.

Time for a Checkup

Can you recite the lyrics of any new song you've heard in the last month?

Can you hum the melody of any piece you've heard in the last month?

When was the last time you "broke into dance" when you listened to music at home?

CUT OUT NUISANCE NOISE

Ads push the principle of noise all the way to the plateau of persuasion. They are quite in accord with the procedures of brainwashing.—MARSHALL MCLUHAN, *Understanding Media,* 1964

A happy life must be to a great extent a quiet life, for it is only in an atmosphere of quiet that true joy can live.
—BERTRAND RUSSELL

I have often lamented that we cannot close our ears with as much ease as we can our eyes.—RICHARD STEELE

On any given day at eleven o'clock in the morning if you walk down the hallway or through the lobby of the average office building, you'll hear ringing phones, beeping pagers, fax machines, laughter, angry voices, music, delivery trolleys and trucks. On the street, the cacophony includes traffic, yelling kids, street vendors, airplanes, and wind. At home, the background fills with arguments, TV jingles, late-breaking news, radio or CD music, slamming doors, running water, swirling fans, the dryer, the dishwasher, the trash compactor, the dustbuster, the razor, ringing phones, doorbells, clanging toys.

Noise produces stress; noise robs you of reflective soothing solitude.

TIME FOR A CHECKUP

Does your TV stay on with no one watching it?

Do your kids do homework to music?

Would neighbors call the police to check on you if things were suddenly quiet?

FEEL THE AWARENESS OF JOY AND GRATITUDE

It is not how much we have, but how much we enjoy, that makes happiness.—CHARLES SPURGEON

Be content with what you have.—HEBREWS 13:5

Nothing should be prized more highly than the value of each day.—JOHANN WOLFGANG VON GOETHE

"They call it take-home pay because there's no other place you can afford to go with it." Such quips are seemingly rather harmless, but some people become embittered—and unbalanced—by such sentiments. A focus on what we *lack,* rather than what we have, produces discontent.

An acquaintance called me recently just to chat, and in the course of the conversation he complained about what a small bonus he'd received from his company upon the successful completion of a long project. Then, almost sounding embarrassed, he caught himself and recanted, "But after all, it was a *bonus*—not something they'd owed me."

Another friend of mine, a flight attendant affected by a strike at a major airline, had this to say about her recent change of attitude: "I was just like the rest of them—griping and complaining before the layoff. But after eight months as a single parent of two teens, since I got hired back, I've got a new disposition at work. They tell me to do something, and I think, 'Sure, I'll be glad to—whatever you ask.' Nothing like scrambling for eight months to teach you to appreciate a paycheck."

Gratitude is a matter of attitude. Perseverance and gratefulness may play as much a part in our lives as talent and reward.

At the age of 38, Johann Sebastian Bach had to compete with five others for the job of choirmaster at Saint Thomas Church, Leipzig. He got the job—not because of his already growing musical reputation, but because he alone agreed to teach Latin five days a week to elementary-age children in the church school!

Gratitude and joy spring from awareness. Some people seem to sleepwalk through life without noticing the moments of true joy. On various ordinary occasions—such as enjoying a holiday meal at my parents' home with all my family gathered around the table, such as when my husband brings me a hot cup of tea brewed with love, such as hearing someone say some thought in some essay changed their life, such as holding a dew-covered rose in my hand—I've been moved to tears about how wonderful life is.

To capture such feeling every day, we have to learn to interpret thoughts, feelings, signs, wishes, and body language of those around us. We have to admit awe and power when we see it. We have to feel humility.

This is not only the stuff of writers and poets. My cattle rancher brother wrote a poem to his daughter, Leanne, on the occasion of her high school graduation last year. No, it will never make a poetry anthology, but it captures well the overwhelming awe of seeing your own flesh-and-blood grow into adulthood.

Does your life seem to be one long, drawn-out sigh? If so, awareness and gratitude can make life's predicaments more palatable.

TIME FOR A CHECKUP

Have you ever felt so emotionally strong about an issue that you composed a poem, a song, or a dance to express yourself?

Have you ever visited the intensive care unit of a hospital or nursing home and found someone with whom you'd like to exchange places?

When is the last time you uttered a prayer of gratitude?

FOCUS ON THE
FAITH FACTOR

I have come that they might have life, and that they may have it more abundantly.—JOHN 10:10

Man would sooner have the void for his purpose than be void of purpose.—FRIEDRICH NIETZSCHE

If a man is to live a full life, an appropriate amount of physical activity must be mixed with mental activity and spiritual activity. Without the existence of spiritual activity, man's life would be void. Without mental activity, man would be numb. Without physical activity, man would be vegetable.—LINUS DOWELL

Americans typically pray. In a 1992 *Newsweek* survey, 91 percent of women and 85 percent of men said they pray regularly. For them, prayer offers calmness and satisfaction. People who neglect the spiritual part of their being feel empty and unbalanced. Emptiness is stressful. Those who have no faith sometimes envy others who seem meaningfully engaged in the pursuit of spiritual things. Rather than ask those people about the source of their meaning or investigate spiritual issues themselves, these people mistakenly try to fill their time with activities—see more art, attend more concerts, donate more time or money to charity.

Faith in God gives me and many other people from all walks of life the sense of . . . purpose in life larger than eating, sleeping, working, playing, reading, relaxing, or relating. Their faith is the fulcrum between feelings of balance and burnout.

TIME FOR A CHECKUP

Have you updated and personalized the beliefs passed on to you in childhood?

Could you write your life's mission in a sentence or two?

KEEP A CLEAR CONSCIENCE

I value people with a conscience. It's like a beeper from God.
—ROBERT ORBEN

We live in deeds, not years; in thoughts, not figures on a dial. We should count time by heart throbs. He most lives who thinks most, feels the noblest, acts the best.—PHILIP BAILEY

Nothing is a better tranquilizer than a clear conscience.
—BANKING (*magazine*)

When a person feels that his thinking is getting broader, it is more likely that his conscience is stretching.—GRIT

Ethical dilemmas and failures can sap the joy out of an otherwise productive day. For starters on a clear conscience and a clean bill of ethics, try this checklist:

- Have you ever padded a résumé?
- Have you ever gossiped about why someone left a job?
- Have you intentionally given the wrong impression about an individual or competitor by what you said or left unsaid?
- Have you ever taken credit for someone else's ideas or accomplishments, passing them off as your own?
- Have you ever pouted, complained, or wished bad things for others because of their promotion, bonus, award, or recognition?

■ Have you ever stolen—time, products, services—
from your employer?

Excuses such as these do not hold up: "But she was
clearly in the wrong." "But he doesn't even know about
it." "It was such a minor thing." "Everybody does it."
"How could anyone possibly be hurt?" "They've done
worse to other people."

How do you deal with the dilemma of a stressed
conscience that leaves you feeling unbalanced? Ask forgiveness and offer forgiveness. Do whatever it takes to
make things right. You'll gain emotional freedom and
peace of mind.

TIME FOR A CHECKUP

*Do you have a "deal" or "situation" at work that
keeps popping into the back of your mind, causing
you to feel guilty?*

*Would you be embarrassed if either your boss, your
best friend, your parent, your child, or your clergy
found out about this troubling deal or situation?*

*Imagine your life being videotaped and played back
for your mother.*

GET OFF THE PAVEMENT AND CONNECT WITH NATURE

Nature, time and patience are the three great physicians.
—Anonymous

Do you remember memorizing these lines from Joyce Kilmer's poem: "I think that I shall never see/a poem lovely as a tree"?

The poet comes as close as any to capturing the beauty and power of nature. Power to make us feel alive again. Power to create gratitude and improve attitude. Power to make us feel one with the universe. When you're feeling down, get away from everything that's artificial and open your senses. Touch a tree. Roll in the grass. Smell the rain. Watch the sunrise. Pet a dog. Hear the crickets. Walk in the sunlight. Shuffle in the snow. Face the wind.

TIME FOR A CHECKUP

How often does your foot touch real dirt?

When is the last time you held a living green leaf in your hand?

Can you see the sunset or sunrise from any place within 3 miles of your home?

GRIND AWAY
AT GREED

The secret of contentment is knowing how to enjoy what you have and being able to lose all interest in things beyond your reach.—ANONYMOUS

I like to walk about amidst the beautiful things that adorn the world; but private wealth I should decline, or any sort of personal possessions, because they would take away my liberty.
—GEORGE SANTAYANA

For where your treasure is, there your heart will be also.
—LUKE 12:34

For a man's life consists not in the abundance of the things which he possesses.—LUKE 12:15

There is no greater calamity than lavish desires. There is no greater guilt than discontent. And there is no greater disaster than greed.—LAO TZU

Do you possess your possessions, or do your possessions possess you? Do you spend every spare moment painting, insuring, cutting, trimming, moving, washing, waxing, polishing, trading, refurbishing, repairing, or storing what you already have? Is it really true that he who dies with the most toys wins?

How rich is rich? You can be too rich when your jewelry spends more time in the bank's safe than on your body. You can be too rich when everything you own needs to be dry-cleaned. You can be too rich when your parakeets have breeding papers. You can be too rich when your chauffeurs must hire assistants. You can be too rich when your distant relatives read the daily obituary columns of your city's newspapers.

Most of us do have serious difficulty in drawing the line between enough and too much. Money won't buy happiness—or so we quote glibly in moments of reflection or during a seminar on values. But our activities sometimes say differently. When we're feeling down, we go to the movies, go shopping, or take a vacation. All of which require money.

Money buys us sightseeing, sleep, security, and status.

If you get swept away in collecting more and more things in early adulthood while traveling toward a successful career, you can wake up one morning in midlife feeling as though you packed for the wrong trip.

You are trading time and energy for money. Is it a happy trade-off for you?

TIME FOR A CHECKUP

Do you wax and wash your car more than you drive it for pleasure?

Do you have clothes stored away throughout an entire season without wearing them?

Do you take exotic vacations that bore and tire you?

Does your sports equipment outclass your skill?

Do you belong to clubs whose services you haven't used in three months?

CUT YOUR EXPENSES

LIVE WITHIN YOUR MEANS

That man is richest whose pleasures are the cheapest.
—HENRY DAVID THOREAU

Time is like money; the less we have of it to spare the further we make it go.—JOSH BILLINGS

Can anyone remember when the times were not hard and money not scarce?—RALPH WALDO EMERSON

About the time we think we can make ends meet, someone moves the ends.—HERBERT HOOVER

Don't equate "living within your means" as deprivation. Instead, think of the income-outgo ratio as balancing your budget against your time.

What do expenses have to do with balance and time? We've become so caught up in the hectic pace that we don't even have time to take care of the money we have. We trash broken items rather than spend the time to take them in for repairs.

Consider other evidence of our attitude of get-more-never-mind-what-we-have: People don't count their change before they walk away from a checkout register. Families don't check their phone bills for errors on long-distance charges. Employers don't audit their 800 numbers for unauthorized use. We slap more stamps than we need on an envelope rather than take the time to locate correct stamps. We pay more for a gift than we intend to pay because we don't have time to walk to a competitor's store. We order from a catalog and pay shipping charges rather than drive to the nearest store. We pay for food prepackaged for six and toss out the two extra servings rather than cook from scratch the correct amount.

Steven Catlin, in his book *Work Less & Play More*, divides our purchases into seven categories: need, investment, pleasure, convenience, ego, tradition, guilt. The first step in making a wise purchase is determining the motivating factor: Do you need the item, or are you buying it because your colleagues have one? Are you buying the toys because your child needs one more toy to learn her numbers, or because you stayed at the office all weekend? Are you sending out Christmas cards because you've *always* sent out Christmas cards? Are you blowing the budget on a big wedding because neighbor Tillie sent her wedding party on a cruise?

Here are some guidelines that may help you cut expenses—both necessary and unnecessary:

- Know your motivation for buying.
- Do not buy on impulse. Establish a waiting period to determine if the need still seems urgent or the deal still seems sound. (If you truly need something, you'll have planned a special trip to the store for that specific purpose.)

- Pay attention to a sale item only if you planned to buy the item anyway.

- Don't buy the superduper edition of something if you don't need and won't use the frills.

- Consider the hidden cost in items you purchase (insurance, registration fees, maintenance, storage, lessons, taxes, shipping).

- Measure the price of purchases in wages and hours required to purchase them.

- Think in terms of cost per use. (Divide the cost of items by the number of times you'll use them. So far, our seven-year-old ski boat has cost $720 per trip to the lake.)

- Don't buy something on a credit card that you don't have money in the bank to cover.

- Make sure you'll stay with the hobby before sinking in hard cash for lessons, equipment, and clothes.

- Use Pareto's 80/20 rule for deciding what an item is worth. Are you spending 80 percent of your food budget for the week on one dining-out meal and then eating like a pauper on the other 20 percent for the week? Are you spending 80 percent of your entertainment budget for one week's vacation, and using the other 20 percent for your amusement activities the remainder of the year? Are you spending 80 percent of your clothing budget on one coat, and wearing the same coveralls every weekend for around-the-house work?

- Teach your kids your guidelines for making wise purchases so they learn to work with rather than buck the system.

- Make a game of finding the "hook" in ads and jingles.
- Don't make shopping a cure for depression.

If you decide that a simpler, more balanced life will bring you more satisfaction than what long hours and more money can buy, then here are some ways to reduce your living expenses:

- Move to a cheaper neighborhood.
- Arrange to live together as an extended family (with parents or children) and share housing costs.
- Observe your daily habits for ways to reduce utilities (using hot water, turning off lights, washing fewer loads of clothes, watering the lawn less frequently, keeping the thermostat set a few degrees higher or lower).
- Entertain yourself with no-cost or low-cost activities.
- Cut your grocery bill by refusing to buy junk food, by buying in quantity, by cooking rather than paying for the convenience of opening a package.
- Plan your purchases so that you can take advantage of regular seasonal sales.
- Buy staples (food, paper goods, health and beauty items) in bulk.
- Live closer to your work so that you can walk or travel to and from work more cheaply.
- Enjoy your time off at home rather than taking exotic trips.
- Entertain your friends and family simply, at home.
- Use things until they wear out.
- Color code clothes. Buy coordinates that you can mix and match.

- Buy decorator items in the same family of colors so that you can use a chair, a vase, a lamp, or a pillow in more than one room.

- Don't buy the best quality for clothes that your children will outgrow before they outwear.

- Don't buy the best quality for items that you will use a limited number of times.

- Make gifts rather than buy them.

- Barter services with friends and neighbors (printing jobs, haircuts, landscaping, babysitting, and so forth).

- Swap items in your home that you no longer have use for or have grown tired of seeing around.

- Buy used items that are in good condition and still have plenty of life in them.

- Recycle things.

- Wait as long as possible to purchase new items on the market; price will come down, and quality will improve.

Your kids will catch on and you'll be rescuing the next generation from living beyond their means and trading valuable time for useless and joyless possessions and habits.

TIME FOR A CHECKUP

Are you paying off your credit card balances in full at the end of each month?

Do you check your monthly bills to make sure all purchases are yours?

Do you go shopping as a pastime?

Are you working two jobs just to pay the bills?

Are you paying people for personal services to do tasks that you'd enjoy doing for yourself if you had the time?

Are you spending money as a status symbol?

BE SOULFUL

The value of life lies not in the length of days, but in the use we make of them; a man may live long yet live very little.
—Montaigne

Without work, all life goes rotten, but when work is soulless, life stifles and dies.—Albert Camus

What lies behind us and what lies before us are tiny matters compared to what lies within us.—Ralph Waldo Emerson

Time is the Life of the Soul.—Henry Wadsworth Longfellow

In past years, more people received more satisfaction on the job because they completed an entire job and saw the results of that job. Mrs. Baird baked the bread, smelled it, delivered it, and saw the smiles on her customers' faces. Today we work in jobs to make products and perform services for customers that we never see. And if your job involves feasibility studies, budgeting, or computer reports, you may have a difficult time even envisioning the big-picture use of your piece of the work pie.

It often surprises me to hear people say, "I hate to eat alone." Or, "I never go shopping alone." When you consider your job mindless or soulless, regain your balance by being your own best customer. Enjoy your own company.

Learn to welcome solitude and work on your inner being—your character. Solitude allows you opportunity to think deep thoughts. To think about where you've been. To think about where you're going. To think about why you feel so strongly about certain issues. To think about how different your values are from those of other people you know. To think about what all people have in common. To question yourself about why you cling to bad habits. To praise yourself for your strengths. To challenge yourself to follow your dreams.

Reflection and solitude feed the soul.

TIME FOR A CHECKUP

Do you enjoy or dread being alone?

Do you direct your thoughts or let your mind roam free when you have an opportunity to be alone?

When do you get your most creative thoughts?

When do you feel the most joyful?

REFOCUS OFTEN

The secret of success is constancy of purpose.
—BENJAMIN DISRAELI

To be what we are and to become what we are capable of becoming is the only end of life.—ROBERT LOUIS STEVENSON

Continually update your activities to match your personal goals and values.

Continually question your decisions to trade time for money and vice versa.

Learn to change your mind as you gather new information.

Eliminate self-defeating patterns of thought and behavior.

Envision and then prepare for what you want.

Do not let yourself think in terms of what others think.

Do not let yourself think in terms of limitations and restrictions of circumstances.

Build strong bridges between yourself and other people.

Adapt your thinking to include the dreams, plans, and values of significant people in your life.

Accept praise for what you have done.

Share credit for the good that has come into your life.

Show gratitude and humility.

Feed your mental, emotional, physical, and spiritual hungers.

Assume responsibility for your time, your life, and your future.

OTHER RESOURCES BY DIANNA BOOHER

BOOKS

Communicate with Confidence: How to Say it Right the First Time and Every Time

The Complete Letterwriter's Almanac

Clean Up Your Act: Effective Ways to Organize Paperwork and Get It Out of Your Life

Cutting Paperwork in the Corporate Culture

Executive's Portfolio of Model Speeches for all Occasions

First Thing Monday Morning

Would You Put That in Writing?

Good Grief, Good Grammar

The New Secretary: How to Handle People as Well as You Handle Paper

Send Me a Memo: A Handbook of Model Memos

To the Letter: A Handbook of Model Letters for the Busy Executive

Writing for Technical Professionals

Winning Sales Letters

67 Presentation Secrets to Wow Any Audience

VIDEOTAPES

Basic Steps for Better Business Writing (series)

Business Writing: Quick, Clear, Concise

Closing the Gap: Gender Communication Skills
Cutting Paperwork: Management Strategies
Cutting Paperwork: Support Staff Strategies

AUDIOTAPE SERIES

Get Your Book Published
People Power
Write to the Point: Business Communications from Memos
to Meetings

SOFTWARE (FLOPPY DISKS AND CD-ROM)

Effective Writing
Effective Editing
Good Grief, Good Grammar
More Good Grief, Good Grammar
Model Business Letters
Model Personal Letters
Model Sales Letters
Model Speeches and Toasts

For More Information

Dianna Booher and her staff travel internationally, speaking and presenting seminars and training workshops on the following communication and motivational topics:
Booher Consultants, Inc.
4001 Gateway Drive
Colleyville, TX 76034-5917
Telephone: 817-540-2678
E-mail: 74107,3347@Compuserve.com

WORKSHOPS

Effective Writing

Technical Writing

Developing Winning Proposals

Good Grief, Good Grammar

Customer Service Communications

Get the Paperwork Off Your Desk

Presentations That Work (oral presentations)

People Power

People Productivity (interpersonal skills)

Listening Until You Really Hear

Resolving Conflict Without Punching Someone Out

Leading and Participating in Productive Meetings

Negotiating So That Everyone Feels Like a Winner

SPEECHES

Get a Life Without Sacrificing Your Career

Putting Together the Puzzle of Personal Excellence

The Plan and Purpose—Despite the Pain and the Pace

Communication: From Boardroom to Bedroom

Communication: The 10Cs

The Gender Communication Gap: "Did You Hear What I Think I Said?"

Communicating CARE to Customers

Write This Way to Success

Platform Tips for the Presenter

INDEX

About the Author

Dianna Booher is an internationally recognized business communications expert and the author of 28 books, including *Communicate with Confidence!*, also published by McGraw-Hill. She is founder and president of Booher Consultants, which has offices in Dallas and Houston. Among her clients are NASA, the Department of the Army, and many Fortune 500 companies, including IBM, Exxon, Mobil Oil, Frito-Lay, US West, Sara Lee, and Pennzoil.